THIS
IS WAR

Also by Hannah Moscovitch:

Bunny
East of Berlin
Infinity
Little One & Other Plays
The Mill Part II: The Huron Bride
The Russian Play and Other Works

THIS
IS WAR

HANNAH
MOSCOVITCH

PLAYWRIGHTS CANADA PRESS | BANFF CENTRE PRESS
TORONTO | BANFF

This Is War © Copyright 2013 by Hannah Moscovitch

PLAYWRIGHTS CANADA PRESS
202-269 Richmond St. W., Toronto, ON M5V 1X1
416.703.0013 ◆ info@playwrightscanada.com ◆ www.playwrightscanada.com

BANFF CENTRE PRESS
The Banff Centre, Box 1020, Banff, AB T1L 1H5
403.762.6410 ◆ press@banffcentre.ca ◆ www.banffcentrepress.ca

For professional or amateur production rights, please contact:
Ian Arnold at Catalyst TCM
310-100 Broadview Ave., Toronto, ON M4M 3H3
416.645.0935 ◆ info@catalysttcm.com

Jacket design by Kisscut Design
Book design by Blake Sproule

LIBRARY AND ARCHIVES CANADA CATALOGUING IN PUBLICATION
Moscovitch, Hannah, author
        This is war / Hannah Moscovitch.

A play.
Co-published by: Banff Centre Press.
Issued in print and electronic formats.
ISBN 978-1-77091-165-9 (pbk.).--ISBN 978-1-77091-166-6 (pdf).--
ISBN 978-1-77091-167-3 (epub)

        I. Title.

PS8626.O837T45 2013   C812'.6   C2013-904398-5
                                                C2013-904399-3

First edition: August 2013. Third printing: July 2018.
Printed and bound in Canada by Imprimerie Gauvin, Gatineau

FSC
www.fsc.org
MIX
Paper from
responsible sources
FSC® C100212

We acknowledge the financial support of the Canada Council for the Arts—which last year invested $153 million to bring the arts to Canadians throughout the country—the Ontario Arts Council (OAC), the Ontario Media Development Corporation, and the Government of Canada for our publishing activities.

 Canada Council   Conseil des arts
for the Arts   du Canada

 ONTARIO ARTS COUNCIL
CONSEIL DES ARTS DE L'ONTARIO
an Ontario government agency
un organisme du gouvernement de l'Ontario

 Canadä

 Ontario
Ontario Media Development
Corporation

For my dear ones, my dear friends Michelle
Murphy, Michael Rubenfeld, and Jill Tomac.

PREFACE

Drama has always been a key component of The Banff Centre's programming. In its founding year of 1933, at the height of the Great Depression, a two-week program in drama was offered to 190 students. Only a few years later, in 1935, playwriting was officially added to the programs on offer. Because of this history, in preparation for the Centre's seventy-fifth year of continuous operation, it felt appropriate to commission a new play to celebrate the Centre's legacy of commitment to the arts and artists; a play that would illustrate the interests and concerns of playwrights in the early years of a new century. More than eighty submissions on a vast array of subjects were received from across Canada, and in April of 2008, Linda Gaboriau, Maureen Labonté, John Murrell, Brian Quirt, and Bob White joined me to select the recipient of the anniversary commission.

While the task was daunting given the overwhelming richness and quality of the proposed works, the terms of the commission helped to identify a clear favourite: Daniel MacIvor proposed a play that would be a departure for him as a playwright, larger in scope and scale than much of his previous work. *Arigato, Tokyo* was to be a play about a Canadian writer communicating with a new audience, challenging his understanding of human and cultural differences, and challenging himself as a man and as an artist on a global stage. It has evolved into a play that is exacting, intensely theatrical, and enormously human. It was a good match with the anniversary celebration and a unanimous choice for the jury.

Fortunately, and happily, the discussions and deliberations did not end there. Despite the breadth of subject matter among the submissions overall, several playwrights responded to Canada's involvement in the war in Afghanistan. Colleen Murphy proposed *Armstrong's War*, a play about the consequences of serving under combat conditions and focusing on a soldier's return to Canada. Hannah Moscovitch proposed *This Is War*, a play about the immediate effects of battle on the men and women of our armed forces, but, like Colleen, her interest was much broader. Hannah's play also explores some of the messy human aspects of modern combat, from the difficulty of knowing the enemy to the psychological impact inflicted upon soldiers on the same side of the conflict.

These were powerful ideas advanced by gifted writers working within a genre that is underrepresented in theatrical literature in this country: the Canadian war play. It seems strange that the performing arts discourse around Canada as a nation at war is largely confined to the media and the political sphere. Enabling these writers to create and develop these plays would contribute to the conversation about Canada's role as a warrior nation within the public arena of the theatre.

And so it was that with a little budget juggling and creative schedule manoeuvring, the anniversary commission provided the opportunity for three plays to be created. With the active co-operation of the Banff Playwrights Colony, first directed by Maureen Labonté and now led by Brian Quirt, and with reading and workshop opportunities in Banff and Toronto, both *This Is War* and *Arigato, Tokyo* have been produced in critically acclaimed premieres in Toronto, at the Tarragon Theatre and at Buddies in Bad Times Theatre, respectively (with more productions planned), while Colleen Murphy's play is scheduled to premiere at the Arts Club Theatre Company in Vancouver in October 2013.

We are thrilled to share these plays with you in partnership with our friends at Playwrights Canada Press, and look forward to many more opportunities to showcase the rich diversity of the dramatic arts in Canada.

Kelly Robinson
Director of Theatre Arts
The Banff Centre
2013

This Is War was first produced at the Tarragon Theatre Extra Space, Toronto, on January 3, 2013, with the following cast and creative crew:

Master Corporal Tanya Young: Lisa Berry
Sergeant Stephen Hughes: Ari Cohen
Sergeant Chris Anders: Sergio Di Zio
Private Jonny Henderson: Ian Lake

Director: Richard Rose
Set and costume design: Camellia Koo
Lighting design: Rebecca Picherack
Composition and sound design: Thomas Ryder Payne
Stage manager: Nicola Benidickson

PUNCTUATION NOTE

Dash (—): A dash at the end of a line of dialogue indicates a cut-off.

Dash 2 (—): A dash in the middle a line of dialogue indicates a quick change in thought or a stutter.

Dash 3 (—dialogue—): Dashes amidst a line of dialogue indicates a person who is speaking over the other character or trying to interrupt the other character.

Ellipsis (…): An ellipsis at the end of a line indicates a trail-off.

Ellipsis 2 (…): An ellipsis in the middle of a line indicates a hesitation or a mental search for a thought or a word.

Slash (/): Indicates the point at which the character that speaks next interrupts the character that is currently speaking.

Beat: Approximately a one-count.

Pause: Approximately a three-count.

Silence: Approximately a six-count.

TERMINOLOGY

In the interests of audience comprehension, terminology was occasionally modified, nor were military terms and slang used in every case. Below is a brief glossary of some of the terms used in the play.

Afghan National Army (ANA): The main branch of the military of Afghanistan, currently being trained by NATO Forces.

Air support: Assistance given to ground troops by their own or allied aircraft.

Black Hawk: A military helicopter, often deployed as MEDEVACS.

Casualty: In military usage, a person who has been either injured or killed.

Comms: Military slang for communication system.

Compound: Either an Afghan house or a fortified Taliban position.

Debrief: An exchange of information about a completed operation.

Foot patrol: A small tactical unit sent out from a larger unit for the purpose of combat, reconnaissance, or a combination of both.

Forward Operating Base (FOB): A secured forward military position, used to support tactical operations. The exterior wall, made up of HESCOS or barbed wire, includes watchtowers and gates.

Fraternization policy: By which no romantic liaisons are permitted between members of the Canadian Forces while on active duty.

Halliburton girls: Halliburton is one of the main suppliers of goods and services to the American military, and so they send employees of the company to Kandahar Airfield who interact, sometimes romantically, with the soldiers stationed at the airfield.

Handset: Contains the receiver and the transmitter on a military radio.

HESCO: A military fortification made of a collapsible wire mesh container and heavy-duty fabric liner, and used as a temporary to semi-permanent barrier against explosions or small-arms fire.

Higher: A military slang term used to describe commissioned officers.

Improvised Explosive Device (IED): A homemade bomb.

International Security Assistance Force (ISAF): The NATO-led security mission in Afghanistan that was established by the United Nations Security Council in December 2001.

Joint operation (joint op): Military actions conducted by the joint forces of two or more armies.

Kandahar Airfield (KAF): One of Afghanistan's largest military bases and the main ISAF base, located sixteen kilometres southeast of the city of Kandahar.

Kevlar: Bulletproof material worn by soldiers in the Canadian Forces.

Kit: The military term for gear.

Master Corporal: A junior non-commissioned officer, second in command to a sergeant in a section of soldiers.

MEDEVAC: A medical evacuation, used to refer to the helicopter performing the evacuation.

Medic: Military personnel who are responsible for providing first aid and front-line trauma care on the battlefield. Combat medics are normally located with the combat troops they serve in order to easily move with the troops and monitor ongoing health concerns.

Nine-liner: Nine lines of information that troops provide to the Tactical Operation Centre to send to the MEDEVAC helicopter coming to collect casualties. A description of the nine lines of information are footnoted on page 34.

Platoon: A military unit typically composed of two to four sections containing twenty-six to sixty-four soldiers.

Private: The lowest military rank.

Resup: Military slang for resupply.

Role 3: The military hospital located at Kandahar Airfield.

Section: A small army unit comprised of eight to ten soldiers in the Canadian Forces, led by a sergeant with a master corporal as second in command.

Sergeant (Sarge): A senior non-commissioned officer rank in the Canadian Forces who acts as section commander. A rank above master corporal.

Tactical Vest (Tac Vest): A military ballistic vest.

Terp: Military slang for interpreter.

PLAYWRIGHT'S NOTE

Between 2007 and 2011 I was talking to soldiers and war correspondents about the experiences of our troops in Panjwaii for a CBC radio show I was writing for called *Afghanada*. I was listening to how soldiers spoke about combat, how they described making life-and-death decisions. One sergeant said to me: "You make the call you think you can live with." That stayed with me. Then a war journalist told me about a combat operation against the Taliban that involved NATO Forces and Afghan Forces. He forwarded me a photograph of the bunker where the incident took place. The play is very loosely inspired by that incident.

CHARACTERS

Master Corporal Tanya Young (late twenties)
Private Jonny Henderson (twenty years old)
Sergeant Stephen Hughes (early to mid thirties)
Sergeant Chris Anders (early to mid thirties)

"We want you guys to see; we want everybody to see what happens to us," one exhausted soldier said. His face was blank, but his eyes were angry.

—Murray Brewster, Defense Correspondent in Afghanistan, *The Canadian Press*

We've shot an amazing number of people...

—General Stanley McChrystal

(This statement was made during an interview with *Rolling Stone* magazine, issued in July of 2010. The general was speaking about the number of Afghan civilian casualties during his time serving as commander of the International Security Assistance Force and American Forces in Afghanistan. Immediately following the *Rolling Stone* interview the general tendered his resignation.)

I find combat, the actual process of pulling the trigger and exploding things and killing people, to be very far removed from any agenda. Whatsoever. Once you've entered that interaction, it's black and white, it's kill or be killed, right, and so, that has nothing to do with anything you believe.

—A soldier, *Operation Homecoming: Writing the Wartime Experience*

I don't know who I killed. I fired into many villages because they were shooting at us. I don't know if I killed anyone that wasn't supposed to be killed—and that haunts me. I can't stop thinking about it, what I've done in my life, what I did there. So, you know, I don't want God to think bad about me, even though I did bad things.

—O'Byrne, airborne infantry, *Infidel* by Tim Hetherington

PART ONE—THIS IS WAR

The soldiers speak directly to the audience. They speak as though a journalist is interviewing them, as though they are responding to interview questions. The conceit in Part One is that the interviews were conducted separately and what we are watching are pieces of the interviews that have been edited together by the journalist. Canadian Forces soldiers are (very generally speaking) wary of, or hostile to, journalists. This hostility takes many forms.

The play takes place in 2007/2008, during the period of the war in Afghanistan when the Canadian Forces were holding Panjwaii, one of the most volatile regions of Afghanistan, with very little support from NATO/ISAF.

Time, place, and memory in the play are created with lights, sound, props, and small furniture. There is minimal or no set.

There are three discrete light boxes that act as the "interview present." The light boxes also establish the interview space itself and define the three interviews as being conducted separately. Sergeant Stephen HUGHES, Private JONNY Henderson, and Master Corporal TANYA Young are in the light boxes. Perhaps we see the three interview subjects waiting for the interviews to start, killing time in small ways, coping with nerves. Or perhaps the lights snap up.

SGT. STEPHEN HUGHES:
It's probably hard for you to get a sense of what it's like on the ground.

PTE. JONNY HENDERSON:
Uh dust.

MCPL. TANYA YOUNG:
Dust.

PTE. JONNY HENDERSON:
I had dust
I kid you not
Plastered to my balls
Plastered.

SGT. STEPHEN HUGHES:
Panjwaii?
It's yeah
It's where we've taken the bulk of our casualties
Yeah Canadians
We keep hearing about an American surge
That's supposed to happen at some point but yeah
Till then it's just us in Panjwaii
(*grinning*) Just us and the Taliban.

PTE. JONNY HENDERSON:
When we first got out there
We went on a foot patrol and one of the guys
He got shot in the
Crotch
He bled out just after the chopper showed up
He died right away—well
Not right away.

SGT. STEPHEN HUGHES:
We
Lost a guy the first day so that set the tone.

MCPL. TANYA YOUNG:
It's yeah
Fields
Villages
It's a nice-looking country
I mean
We were calling in air support and

Bombing it so
Right now it looks like shit.

SGT. STEPHEN HUGHES:
There were a couple of villages all pretty close by the camp
We were trying to build relationships there
I was working on my Pashtu
I can say friend
Stop
Hello
I was working on my Pashtu—is this what you want to ask me about?

PTE. JONNY HENDERSON:
The Taliban they uh
They use kids
Kids strapped to IEDs
It's
It'll
If it's packed with nails 'n' uh
Uh scraps
Metal scraps
It'll cut through your Kevlar 'n' fuck up your lungs
Cut up your
Your uh
Your balls.

SGT. STEPHEN HUGHES:
No we weren't peacekeeping
If you're peacekeeping you're trying to keep two hostile groups from fighting each other
In Afghanistan we're
One of the two hostile groups
(*grinning*) Actually we could've used some peacekeepers over there.

PTE. JONNY HENDERSON:
They use kids

Kids like fifteen
Sixteen
Me?
No I'm twenty?

SGT. STEPHEN HUGHES:
The Taliban?
No
No mostly we didn't see them
We'd see a flash
See movement in a treeline
(*leaning forward*) How'd we know it was them?
(*grinning*) Well they'd be firing on us.

MCPL. TANYA YOUNG:
Any fighting-age guy
Any fighting-age guy could be Taliban
You see a weapon
A cellphone
You fire.

SGT. STEPHEN HUGHES:
Yeah they're
They'd get so close to us they could kill one of my guys walk with his weapon
and we still hadn't fucking seen them?
That's yeah
They're yeah
That's
Alarming.

MCPL. TANYA YOUNG:
Yeah sure it happens—we had this one situation with this local
He said to us
There's no one in the compound
No one no people
We went in we saw movement 'n' we fired

And

Pause.

It's his sister
His little sister
His sister is no one.

SGT. STEPHEN HUGHES:
Oh yeah there's not a second you're out there that you're not thinking
They are not
They are not
Kidding
They're not fucking around out there—we're at war

Pause. HUGHES *listens then grins, laughs, and there's a beat here where all three soldiers react to the question. Perhaps* JONNY *and* TANYA *give the interviewer a blank or guarded look, prepare themselves to answer the difficult part of the interview, and we're focused on all three of them.*

I've been waiting for you to get to that

Beat.

No
No

Beat. He shrugs.

You can ask me that again the answer's still fucking "no."

PTE. JONNY HENDERSON:
No we didn't see it.

MCPL. TANYA YOUNG:
No

I didn't know what happened
No I didn't know what happened in the bunker.

SGT. STEPHEN HUGHES:
No
We didn't
No
That's the Afghan National Army
They assaulted the compound
We secured the perimeter

He shrugs.

That's a joint operation
You co-operate with local militaries
In this case the ANA who aren't always up on the uh
The finer points of the
Geneva Convention.

MCPL. TANYA YOUNG:
No I didn't hear it.

PTE. JONNY HENDERSON:
No
No
I didn't hear it.

MCPL. TANYA YOUNG:
No no one's stopping me
I can talk to the media
I can say what I did
I can say what I saw

Beat. She shrugs, then, as though this is obvious:

They're the enemy

If they're dead then we did our job.

We hear a sound.

It suggests people being tortured, realizing they're going to die, in the final stages of life, trampling each other. There is nothing normal about this sound; it is not how people sound when they're being tortured on film; it's an animal sound, ugly, foreign, not easily recognizable.

The sound may be naturalistic, or not.

We should have a visceral, involuntary, animal response to the sound.

The sound should make us feel a little sick, but we don't know why.

The soldiers keep looking out at us.

The sound may make them uncomfortable: they shift in their seats or they stare us down blankly.

Perhaps the sound escalates and escalates, hits a crescendo.

Transition.

End of Part One.

PART TWO—INTERVIEW WITH MASTER CORPORAL TANYA YOUNG

Master Corporal TANYA *Young speaks to the audience.*

The conceit is that the audience is a journalist and TANYA *is telling the journalist about the twenty-four hours surrounding the joint operation.*

MCPL. TANYA YOUNG:
Last time a reporter talked to me it was "What's it like being a female in the infantry?"
(leaning forward) What's it like?
What?
You want to know now?
Uhhhhmmmmmmmm
Well I had to learn how to pee in a water bottle
I peed on my hands a lot for a while

TANYA *grins.*

Hey look I'm not gonna lie there are those shitty—excuse me—hard parts of it
Where you think
There's gotta be something else I could
Sell cars or
I joined up to stop being with the wrong people at the
Wrong places so

Beat.

Yeah hard parts like I just told you
I just told you
There was a situation this other time with my section and a civilian casualty

A child
Took fire
And died
It was this local's little sister
The local said to us there was no one in his compound
No one
No people
We went in and saw movement that turned out to be
Her
His sister
Running
Running away from us down a passageway
She was
Five years old this
Girl and
That's not the kind of thing you
Shrug off
That stays with you when you
See it so

Beat.

So is that it that all your questions?

Beat. She leans in to hear the question:

Yeah okay
Uhhhhhh
The night before the joint op with the Afghan National Army we
Played cards
Played for a couple of hours
By oh one hundred it was just the sergeant 'n' me left
Rest of the platoon tapped out they were back in the shacks
Shacks
Yeah like barracks but *shittier*
Uhhh

HUGHES *is there.*

Yeah I don't know what else to tell you I
Played some poker—

Shift: memory.

We're in the camp mess tent at night. HUGHES *and* TANYA *have cards. There's seventy bucks in cash in front of them, in fives.*

HUGHES:
Good hand?

He whistles the tune to "Sunglasses at Night," then:

Couple of aces? What've you got there?

Beat.

Just so you know, I got my qualification in tactical questioning.

TANYA:
Yeah?

HUGHES:
Yep.

TANYA:
Well, just so you know, I'm good at poker.

HUGHES:
So… you've got a good hand?

TANYA *shoots him a look.* HUGHES *grins and then taps his foot, glances at his cards. Meanwhile,* TANYA *is rock still.*

I can't fucking sit still.

TANYA:
(*without looking up*) Yeah, you can't.

HUGHES:
Shut up.

TANYA:
(*without looking up*) You shut up.

Pause. HUGHES *assesses* TANYA *then rubs his eyes and face. He throws his cards down on the table face up.*

TANYA:
Don't... *show me your cards!*

HUGHES:
You win.

TANYA:
No: *pick up your*—pick them up.

TANYA *goes to pick up* HUGHES's *cards and hand them back to him.* HUGHES *gets there first, stops her from giving them back to him.*

Hey! No! Come on: lose like a loser.

HUGHES *flicks the cards at her. They hit* TANYA's *chest and arms.*

You having fun with that?

HUGHES:
Yep.

HUGHES *keeps flicking cards at her, one at a time. Some of them hit her in the chest and the arms. She lets him hit her with the cards, takes it. They look at each other and* HUGHES *stops hitting her with the cards.*

TANYA:
Why are you... looking at me like that...?

HUGHES *shrugs.*

TANYA *pushes her chair back and starts picking the cards up off the floor.* HUGHES *watches her.*

HUGHES:
We could... get it out of our systems, unless I'm talking shit but I don't think it's / just me—

TANYA:
Get it out of your—*are you a virgin?* What the fuck? Does that work? Does that work on... someone: girls, nurses—

HUGHES:
I don't think it's just me.

TANYA:
It's just you, Sarge.

HUGHES:
Oh yeah?

TANYA:
How're we alone?

HUGHES:
They all folded. You gonna hit the sack, or what? You're not gonna hit the sack.

TANYA:
I'm hitting the sack.

HUGHES:
Be a distraction.

TANYA:
From *what?*

HUGHES:
(*intimate*) The shit you're running in your head.

They look at each other. HUGHES *shrugs, looking at her.*

TANYA:
Are you *kidding me—?*

HUGHES:
Well it will.

TANYA:
You're an *asshole.* No—!

HUGHES *is going towards her for the kiss. It's illicit-sexy.* HUGHES *and* TANYA *kiss for a few beats, then:*

This is bad—

HUGHES:
Shut up—

HUGHES *very efficiently pushes or walks* TANYA *back, lays her out on the table. As he does this,* TANYA *is saying:*

TANYA:
No, I mean it, this is bad, this is bad, like—you—no: come on, you're trying to get yourself sent home, you're trying to get me sent home, what are you… doing—are you backing me up?

Pause as HUGHES *kisses her again.*

Someone's going to walk in—

HUGHES:
No they're not—

TANYA:
No: get off me. Get off. No, I mean it.

HUGHES:
You mean it?

Pause. HUGHES *looks at her to see if she means it, hesitates. They both waver: should they do it?*

TANYA:
(low) Uh fuck.

And that decides it. HUGHES *leans in to kiss her or pull her clothes off on the table. There's an escalation of sexuality. Then there's a shift: we're back to the interview.*

MCPL. TANYA YOUNG:
(flustered) Yeah sorry I heard you I'm trying to remember exactly what happened that night
We

Beat.

Nothing

Nothing happened
We played a couple of rounds
Me and the sergeant
I won the game
I used to play with my mom
I used to beat her
My math was better than hers
That and she was always *hammered*
Anyway
It was stupid
Staying up that late
But
It's not like it's easy to sleep
Shacks smell like
There's no showers at camp—there's *wet wipes* times sixty guys
Most nights I lie in there trying not to *barf all over myself* so
I wasn't in a big hurry for the game to end—

Shift: memory.

We're in the mess tent at night, moments later. HUGHES *is testing his knee.* TANYA
is fixing up her clothes.

HUGHES:
My leg hurts. From holding you up. My knee.

TANYA:
Yeah?

HUGHES *is putting weight on his leg, testing it.*

HUGHES:
Shit! My kneecap's over on the side of my leg: see that, look at that, it's
off-centre—

TANYA:
No it's not.

HUGHES:
Yeah, I think I twisted it.

HUGHES tries to stretch out his knee.

Shit! Shit: I blew out my knee; I shouldn't have been... hefting you.

TANYA shoots him a look.

(off TANYA's reaction) What? Oh come on, you're a big girl, you're built, I like built?

Beat.

Hey come on, I'm sorry, I didn't mean to—we good? Hey?

TANYA:
(without looking at him) What?

HUGHES:
We good?

Pause. TANYA is ignoring HUGHES.

Okay: what do you want? Well tell me. Did you... like that? I liked it?

Beat, then HUGHES goes to exit.

(to himself, defensive) I liked it.

HUGHES exits, limping.

(over his shoulder, calling to TANYA) Don't forget your seventy bucks.

Pause as TANYA *looks towards the exit, hears something, and tenses, clocks something happening outside the tent.* TANYA *quickly moves to finish fixing herself up, fixing her clothes. Then she starts picking up any cards left on the ground and throwing them on the table. We half-hear the following dialogue off stage—it's very faint—while we are seeing the above:*

(off stage) Private. Just lost five bucks. Tanya cleaned up. She's in there counting her money. You good? You okay? You gonna smoke that? You okay? Hey, hey, no: let's just—might want to… give her a sec in there. You good, Private? You okay? You look a little…? Jonny, I just said d…

JONNY *enters.*

JONNY:
You still playing?

A beat as TANYA *turns and looks at* JONNY *for a split second to try and work out what he knows.*

TANYA:
Game just ended.

JONNY:
Oh yeah? Who won?

TANYA:
I did.

JONNY:
How much?

TANYA:
Seventy bucks. Why are you up: go to sleep—

JONNY:
(holding up a couple of the bent cards) Did you sit on the fucking cards?

TANYA:
Yeah, I rolled around in them after I won. I'm gonna hit the sack—

JONNY:
Yeah?

TANYA:
Yep.

JONNY:
Wanna play a round with me?

Beat.

TANYA:
I just said I'm tired, I'm gonna / hit the sack.

JONNY:
You wanna play a round with me?

TANYA looks at JONNY.

Then JONNY gets hold of TANYA. JONNY is aggressive about it.

TANYA:
Get... off—

JONNY kisses TANYA forcibly, aggressively. TANYA lets him for a few beats. Then she starts trying to push him off of her.

Get off / me.

JONNY:
Come on.

TANYA:
Get / off!

JONNY:
Come on: what do you care?

TANYA:
Get the fuck off me, Jonny. Jesus.

TANYA pushes him off of her.

Beat while they look at each other.

Don't do that. Come on, buddy. Don't be that guy.

Shift: interview.

MCPL. TANYA YOUNG:
After the poker game I
Stood outside the mess tent didn't even have a smoke on me
Nothing sadder than standing around *not smoking*
Anders
He's one of the medics
He was up too
Night before an op everyone gets a little tweaked—

Shift: memory.

TANYA is outside the mess tent, lit by mess tent fluorescents, in the dark. She's trying to collect herself for a half-second. Perhaps her hands are over her face. ANDERS walks in on this.

ANDERS:
Tanya?

TANYA:
Yeah?

ANDERS:
You... up?

TANYA:
Yeah?

ANDERS:
Why?

TANYA:
Poker game just ended. You got a smoke?

ANDERS:
You still not sleeping?

TANYA:
Can you give me something for it? 'Cause what I'm taking for it isn't working.

ANDERS:
What are you taking for it?

Beat.

You okay?

TANYA:
Yeah, yeah: just... fucking up my life, just—yeah: stupid.

Pause.

ANDERS:
Lot of... assholes in camp?

TANYA:
(*as in "no"*) One per person.

ANDERS:
Okay!

TANYA:
Just can't sleep.

ANDERS:
(*smiling*) You... want me to come sing you a lullaby?

TANYA:
You're not even kidding.

ANDERS:
Yeah, well, you look like crap: I want you to get some sleep.

There is the loud sound of a crate chair being knocked over and stamped on and someone yelling inside the mess tent.

JONNY:
(*off stage*) ...stupid!

ANDERS *looks towards the tent.* TANYA *tenses.* ANDERS *clocks this.*

TANYA:
Jonny's in the mess test.

ANDERS:
Jonny. Okay. I was—I'm gonna... go in there: is that...?

TANYA:
(*defensive*) Yeah...?

ANDERS:
Okay…!

ANDERS walks into the mess tent. TANYA watches this for a beat, worried.

Shift: interview.

MCPL. TANYA YOUNG:
Hit the sack
Couldn't fucking sleep
Excuse my potty mouth but *I couldn't fucking sleep*
Next morning oh five hundred hours I was on sentry with one of the guys in my section

JONNY is there with his C8 rifle. He starts adjusting the crotch of his pants.

With uh
With
With one of the
A guy from my section.

Shift: TANYA and JONNY are on sentry (they are up a tower looking over the HESCOS that make up the perimeter of the forward operating base) holding their C8 rifles. There is a long pause during which JONNY adjusts the crotch of his pants. He adjusts several times and becomes engrossed in adjusting. TANYA glances over a couple of times. Finally—finally—TANYA can't take it anymore.

TANYA:
What's happening down there, buddy?

JONNY:
Balls are sweating.

TANYA:
Oh yeah?

JONNY:
Dripping.

TANYA:
Sounds uncomfortable.

Pause as JONNY keeps adjusting, hands down his pants now.

TANYA's focus is split between the horizon and JONNY's crotch.

Okay, you wanna take that to the can?

JONNY:
It's just my balls are sticking to my… ass: I'm trying to free them up, my gear's getting in my… way, but if I just… adjust my straps, or… wait, no, I think I got 'em, if I just…

(*off* TANYA's *reaction*) What, you never had a pair of balls stuck to your ass? Nice pair of balls? Fifty-degree heat?

TANYA looks away. JONNY wipes his hand on his shirt.

TANYA leans forward, squints at the horizon.

TANYA:
You see that?

JONNY:
What?

TANYA:
One o'clock. Four hundred metres.

JONNY:
Uh yeah.

TANYA:
Call the terp. And call the sarge.

JONNY:
What for?

TANYA:
Hey, call them 'cause I told you to.

Shift: interview.

MCPL. TANYA YOUNG:
That's when we saw two Afghan men walking up towards the gate
They were carrying a boy
He was nine
Ten
Little kid
There was a rag tied round his stomach
It had blood on it

Beat: stress breath.

I was
Agitated about that
I thought
Shit
Their kid's hurt
They're going to be stupid about this
They're not going to stop they're going to walk right up to the gate and we're
going to have to fire on them
On that
Kid.

JONNY is moving up, towards TANYA.

TANYA:
(in the scene) Uh no.

Shift: memory. We're back on sentry at camp.

(calling to the Afghans) No, wait there! Stay back!

JONNY:
(to TANYA) They're coming.

TANYA:
(calling) Stay the fuck—stay back. Just… wait! *(to JONNY)* Where's the terp?

JONNY:
Coming—he's praying.

TANYA:
(squinting at the boy) I just don't want to fire on that… kid—*shit*. How the fuck do you say "Wait there?" Are they picking him up?

JONNY:
No. They're just talking to him. The old guy's crouched down / talking to him.

TANYA:
Yeah, that's why I think he might be picking him back up.

JONNY:
They're not.

TANYA:
(calling) Fuck—stay there! Stay back!!!!

JONNY:
They're not picking him up.

TANYA:
Then what the hell are they doing?!!!

JONNY:
Talking to him!

Then, seeing HUGHES on his way over from off stage:

Sergeant's coming. His Pashtu's pretty good. Hey, he's "working on his Pashtu." He can say "goat" and "friend" and… "goat."

JONNY grins at her.

TANYA turns away.

TANYA watches the kid, the Afghan men, and gets more and more agitated. JONNY starts watching the kid. Periodically TANYA looks to see if the terp is coming. He's not in sight.

(sincere now, concerned) Poor kid.

Beat.

Kid's not going to make it.

Beat. JONNY leans in.

Those his guts?

TANYA:
Where the fuck's the terp: / what the fuck's happening!!!

JONNY:
He's praying; he's coming!

Beat.

Hey, that terp? He asked me if it's true you're a woman. He should've been outside the mess tent last night, I think that would've... uh...

TANYA has turned and is looking at JONNY.

He clicks at her.

Beat.

Then he asked me if you fuck all of us or just him.

TANYA punches JONNY in the head. He goes down hard, on his ass. HUGHES enters, running, and gets between them, gets hold of TANYA.

Simultaneously:

HUGHES:
(*to TANYA*) Hey! Hey!!!

TANYA:
(*to JONNY*) Don't *touch* me!

JONNY:
I didn't touch you!

HUGHES:
Hey! / Hey, hey!

TANYA:
(*to JONNY, fully losing her shit*) Hey *fuck you, you shitty little kid,* go fuck yourself—

HUGHES:
HEY / HEY—!

TANYA:
—little cherry bitch, fucking prairie boy—

HUGHES:
HEY!

TANYA:
I'm gonna *fucking kill you.*

HUGHES *pulls* TANYA *away from* JONNY. *He stands between* JONNY *and* TANYA, *blocks* TANYA's *view of* JONNY. JONNY *touches his face, sitting on the ground, his back to the audience.*

HUGHES:
(*to* TANYA) Hey! No, look at me. What's going on? Master Corporal?

TANYA *is furious, panting. She shakes her head at* HUGHES.

Okay, go for a walk. Go for a / walk.

TANYA:
Yeah, I'm…! I'm going for a walk.

Shift: interview.

MCPL. TANYA YOUNG:
It took about ten minutes for the terp to show up
The

Stress breath.

The upshot was the boy'd been knifed in the stomach
We asked if it was Taliban they said no
But
The locals don't inform on the Taliban
The

Two men were the boy's
Father and brother-in-law
They'd come
Carried him from their village
The terp's translating this back and forwards meanwhile the kid's lying there
Bleeding out
Twenty metres in front of us
The ground's
There's blood pooling

Beat. She shakes her head. Stress breath.

So that

Pause.

I just didn't want to be watching a little boy bleed out for fifteen minutes in front of the gate it

HUGHES *is there and is looking at* TANYA.

We
Followed standard operating procedure—we got them through the gate
Anders started an IV
Gave the boy morphine
Fluids—

Shift: memory.

HUGHES *has a slight limp in this scene.*

HUGHES:
What was that?

TANYA:
I don't know. I don't know: I lost my temper.

HUGHES:
Yeah: why? What happened? Jonny... say something to you?

TANYA:
No.

HUGHES:
Then why'd you lose your temper?

TANYA:
Uuuuhhhmmm: the heat?

HUGHES:
(*low*) Come on: I'm on your side. I saw him, last night, on my way out of the mess, I thought that was maybe going to go... badly. I should've—*yeah*...

He shakes his head, clicks, pissed off with himself.

What'd he just say to you: he... say something stupid? He... call you a name?

Beat.

How about this: stay at camp. Manage the civilians for the day, calm down—

TANYA:
(*very low*) Hey *fuck you*.

HUGHES:
(*low*) Okay you need to *calm the fuck down.*

ANDERS enters.

ANDERS:
So yeah: it looks like a knife injury to me, that kid's lost a lot of blood. I'm pumping him full of saline but it's not good; it could be a bad day for him: he's gotta go to KAF—am I—am I... interrupting / something?

HUGHES:
No, no.

Beat.

No—

ANDERS:
The kid's got to go to KAF.

HUGHES:
Master Corporal Young's gonna to stay at camp with you.

ANDERS:
Okay...?

Beat. HUGHES *is exiting.* ANDERS *is looking at* TANYA.

Okay?

TANYA:
What.

ANDERS:
What—nothing! Good! Great! I like having you around: what could be better?

Shift: interview.

MCPL. TANYA YOUNG:
That's when I got orders to stay at camp and manage the civilian situation—so like I said I didn't go on the joint op
I can't tell you what happened with the Afghan National Army 'cause I don't know
'Cause I was at camp
The whole day

I don't know I did whatever the fuck I do at camp—I jerked off to Matt
Damon I don't know!

Yeah big Matt Damon fan

Uhhhhh

Bourne Identity?

Yeah you should watch it

Give it a good watch

I don't know!

What the fuck does it matter I was at camp!

I fucking don't

Want to be talking about this!

Shift: memory.

TANYA *is on radio, speaking into a handset, rapid-fire.*

TANYA:
Zero, this is three-two alpha, over. Three-two, requesting immediate
MEDEVAC, over.

Beat.

Roger, nine-line is—break—one: FOB Mahone. Two: 39-39, romeo. Three:
priority one, urgent. Four: "A." Five: "L." Six: "N." Seven: "D." Eight: "D"
and "F" non-coalition civilian casualty, a child. Nine: "N," "I" abdominal
injury, he's lost a lot of blood. "S" difficulty breathing. "T" morphine. Over.*

---

* Below is a description of Tanya's radio chatter and the nine lines of information she references.

Zero is the call sign of the tactical operations centre.
Three-two alpha is Tanya's company, platoon, and section call sign (she is identifying herself).
Line one indicates the location of the pick-up site.
Line two indicates the radio frequency.
Line three indicates the priority level of the casualty. Priority one indicates the injury is to life,
limb, or eyes. It is the highest level of priority.
Line four indicates what special equipment is required. "A" indicates no special equipment
such as a ventilator is required.
Line five indicates if the casualty needs a litter (stretcher), or "L."
Line six indicates security at the pick-up site, or how "hot" the landing zone is. "N" indicates
that there are no enemy troops in the area.

Beat.

Three-two, yeah: non-combat, non-coalition civilian casualty, he's lost a lot of blood—he's a child.

Beat.

Three-two: yeah, I'll wait out.

Pause. TANYA *listens. She closes her eyes as she listens, leans her head against the wall. Through the following there's no emotion.*

Three-two, please acknowledge: the child will die if you don't send.

TANYA *listens for a couple more beats.*

(into the handset, calm) Out.

Then she smashes the handset against a wall, a table: a hard surface. ANDERS *runs in and is trying to get her to give him the handset.*

ANDERS:
HEY!!! HEY!!!!

TANYA *is still smashing the handset.*

HEY DON'T DO THAT!!!

ANDERS *jogs up and pries the handset out of* TANYA's *hand.*

Line seven indicates the method of marking the landing zone. "D" indicates "none," or no markers will be used in this case.
Line eight indicates the casualty's nationality and military status.
Line nine indicates the terrain or enemy obstacles at the landing zone, in this case "N," or none. If there's time, the soldier will supply further information, such as injury sustained, or "I"; symptoms and vital signs, or "S"; and any medications that have been administered to the casualty, or "T," for treatment given.

Give me that. Give it to me. We need that!

ANDERS *takes the handset.*

The hell's going on? HEY!!!

TANYA:
(*calm*) I called in the nine-liner. I… called in the / nine-liner—

ANDERS:
You losing it? What— / What's…?

TANYA:
(*calm*) No, I called in the nine-liner—

ANDERS:
Yeah? And? What? They're held up? They're held up? What? They're not coming?

TANYA:
No, they're not coming!!!

TANYA *goes to push over a table or knock something over.* ANDERS *stops her.*

ANDERS:
Why? No, HEY, HEY! STOP IT! You want me to talk to the family? I'll talk to them.

TANYA:
No. No. I'll talk to the family.

ANDERS:
No, you know what? I'll talk to them.

TANYA:
No, I'll talk to them, I'm fine! Matter of fact, I *love this country.*

Shift: interview.

MCPL. TANYA YOUNG:
(calm) I got on radio
Called in a nine-liner for a chopper to move the kid to Role 3
To the hospital at KAF
The request was denied
The chopper was on standby for the joint op
For
Combat injuries

Beat: stress breath.

But
If you're
Say
Having a bad day
You're just
Having a bad day
And you're looking down at a kid
He's right there
He's lost a lot of blood
He's just a kid
Kids when they're
Bleeding out
They lie very still
They're very brave
They
Blink a lot

Pause.

I went into the medical tent
Pulled the family out
I didn't want the boy to hear
Don't know why kid didn't speak any English

Father must have been fifty
Fifty-five
He'd been carrying the boy for an hour
His arms were shaking
The son-in-law had a lot of blood on his hands
He kept wiping his hands on his
Dress
Robe
I got him some wet wipes
Sat down with them and I said
Uh the kid's name was Mohammed
Mohammed yeah like the *prophet*
I said
"Mohammed's not going to… live more than a few more hours"
They knew
They knew right away I don't know *how*
My tone?
Father stood up
Son-in-law said something in Pashtu
Heard the word Allah
The father was
It was
His son
Then we just waited for that to
We waited.

Shift: memory. ANDERS *has just entered or is entering. Perhaps in this scene we hear the faint and far-off sound of small-arms fire.*

ANDERS:
Okay, Tanya, don't lose it on me, just… try not to lose it—

TANYA:
Why?

ANDERS:
They want to take him. They want to move him. The family—they're—they're picking him up. The IV lines are pulling out—

TANYA:
—so let's—

ANDERS:
—and I can't—no—and I can't… stop them—

TANYA:
Why not?

ANDERS:
'Cause we're not doing anything for him…

TANYA gets up and starts to walk to the exit. ANDERS gets between her and the exit, stops her.

Hey—no—stay here!

TANYA:
No. Where are they going with him?

ANDERS:
I don't know—no! NO!

TANYA is walking towards the exit again. ANDERS blocks her.

No—we're going to let them.

TANYA:
The IV lines are pulling out!

ANDERS:
Yeah they are!

TANYA:
He's a kid!

ANDERS:
(as in "that's absolutely true") Yeah!

Pause: a standoff.

TANYA:
(low) Fine, fuck.

TANYA goes and leans her head back against the wall or sits herself down somewhere.

There's a silence.

ANDERS observes TANYA, considers her.

ANDERS:
You look like... a loaf of crap—you get... *any* sleep last night?

Beat.

So: no.

Beat.

You... looking after yourself?

TANYA:
Yeah?

ANDERS:
Yeah?

TANYA:
Why? What.

Beat.

What.

ANDERS:
He can't get pregnant.

TANYA:
What the fuck!!! How do you know about that?

ANDERS:
How do you think?

TANYA:
How do I... *think?* I don't know?!

ANDERS:
He told me that you and him... had intercourse.

(off TANYA's *reaction)* All right, I'm trying to clean up my language—

TANYA:
Jesus.

ANDERS:
It's not a big deal as long as you're... discreet. And on birth control. Are you? It's not my business—

TANYA:
No fucking kidding.

ANDERS:
You don't have to tell me.

TANYA:
No I don't.

ANDERS:
You've gotta keep that discreet. If you don't want to get sent home, you've gotta keep that discreet or your sergeant's gonna have to do something about it.

TANYA:
Who are you—*what?!* Who are you talking about?

ANDERS:
Jonny.

TANYA:
Jonny.

Beat.

ANDERS:
Okay, Tanya, *what the hell's going on?* Not Jonny? He was in the mess tent… last night—?

TANYA:
What did Jonny say to you?

ANDERS:
He doesn't have to *say anything.* If you're within fifty metres he's got his eyes on you, I've never seen a guy so lovesick; I mean he's young but he's… a good guy, he'd be a good—*who were you talking about?* Someone else? Someone else?

Beat.

Wow, okay, wow, is it who I think it m…? Okay, Tanya, you're—yeah—you're screwing up your life. Why can't you sleep, what are you seeing: you're running all that stuff in your mind, the stuff from our last tour…?

Beat.

It's the stuff with the civilian, from our last tour, the little girl that you fired on.

Beat.

TANYA *shrugs.*

(*as in "this is not good"*) Tanya...!

TANYA:
Yeah.

ANDERS:
You have to... put that away, / you have to...

TANYA:
Yeah, yeah.

Silence.

I... just thought I could... say this kid's a combat injury.

Beat.

ANDERS:
He's not.

TANYA:
(*as in "that's absolutely true"*) Yeah—

ANDERS:
They'll know it's the same one, how'll they not / know that?

TANYA:
Yeah but that might not stop them from sending; he's a kid: they're probably…
feeling bad.

*TANYA walks towards the radio to pick up the handset but ANDERS blocks her
way again.*

Let me—

ANDERS:
No.

TANYA:
—try / that—why not?

ANDERS:
Don't touch that—

TANYA:
Why not?

ANDERS:
—just don't go crazy on me!

Pause.

Both ANDERS and TANYA have their hands on the handset.

TANYA:
(low, rueful) It'd be really good if *one thing* went… good today. That'd be good,
just for… some… variety of… things to have in my brain.

Beat.

Where are they: are they… at the gate by now?

ANDERS:
All right, try it.

ANDERS lets go of the handset.

Shift: interview.

MCPL. TANYA YOUNG:
I
Called in a second nine-liner
Thought "Why the"
"Why the *heck* not"
And hey
They agreed to send
For a second you're like
Good
Good
Get the kid some basic

Beat: stress breath.

Thirteen minutes later the Black Hawk's there
We load the boy in
Him and his family
The father was
(gestures) Saying thank you or
Something in Pashtu that sounded like thank you—

Sound: chopper in the near distance. We're on the landing zone at camp.

Shift: ANDERS is there.

TANYA:
So?

ANDERS:
So?

TANYA:
He looked… pretty shitty?

ANDERS:
He'll be fine.

TANYA:
Yeah?

ANDERS:
Poor kid: that sucked, there, for a few minutes, for him, but yeah, he'll be fine.

Beat.

TANYA:
Well that's good.

ANDERS:
(*grinning*) Yeah!!!

ANDERS *pats* TANYA *on the back.*

TANYA *takes a deep breath.*

Hey: it's almost like you're smiling.

TANYA *flashes him a brief smile.*

Good. Good. Better?

Beat. The sound of the MEDEVAC *chopper in the near distance fades out as a new sound is heard. It's the same sickening sound as in Part One. In the distance somewhere people are hurt. The sound is faint. There is also perhaps the faint and far-off sound of small-arms fire.*

TANYA:
What is that?

ANDERS:
What?

TANYA:
That... sound?

Pause: sound.

They listen.

That animals, or...?

The sound goes on and on, under her interview.

Shift: interview.

TANYA speaks to the audience.

MCPL. TANYA YOUNG:
When my platoon came back

HUGHES is there: he appears like a PTSD hallucination, looking shell-shocked, glassy-eyed, exhausted, with dried and crusted reddish brown blood on his tac vest.

When they came back...

Shift: memory.

HUGHES is about to limp past TANYA at the forward operating base.

TANYA:
Uh you...? Sarge? Sarge?

HUGHES:
(*turning to look at her*) Uh yuh.

TANYA:
Is that yours?

HUGHES:
Uh. No. No: Jonny's at KAF, in surgery.

(*off* TANYA's *reaction*) Yeah: higher's gonna do a debrief. He was... okay for a while—he was cracking jokes. But the chopper took an hour to show up. I was on radio going, "Where the fuck's the chopper." We tried to keep him talking to us. The chopper took its fucking time: took its fucking time, no fucking chopper.

Pause. TANYA *struggles with herself.*

Don't punch the dirt, I've done that, it... hurts—

TANYA:
I called the chopper for the Afghan kid, that's why it didn't come.

HUGHES:
What Afghan kid?

TANYA:
The kid, the kid, the Afghan kid, the civilian kid: the walk-up.

Beat as HUGHES *remembers the kid* TANYA *is talking about, takes that info in.*

HUGHES:
(*very low, dead serious*) Oh yeah?

Beat.

'Kay. Well. I guess you… I don't know: find a way to live with that?

HUGHES *wipes his bloody and dirty hands on his bloody tac vest, still looking at* TANYA. *Then he limps away.*

TANYA *stands there for a moment: she's somewhere between the memory and the present of the interview.*

Perhaps there's a graduated lighting shift.

Then TANYA *speaks to the interviewer.*

MCPL. TANYA YOUNG:
Sorry

She clears her throat.

Excuse me
When
I'm just thinking of when the platoon came back I found out one of the guys in my section
Jonny
He was a
A casualty

Pause as TANYA *tries to pull herself together and not cry.*

TANYA *rubs her eyes.*

Sorry
Sorry I didn't
Get a lot of sleep last night—I'm still staying with my mom on her couch
It's
Stupid I gotta

She has this fridge it clicks on at night it's so freakin' loud it scared the shit
out of me I punched the fridge
Now there's this big
Dent in the
Fridge
I'm taking a
Like a handful of sleeping pills
They don't work—you know what works?
Liquor
Which is *super* 'cause my mom keeps a ton of it in her house

TANYA *rubs her eyes.*

Guess that sounds pretty *fucked up* to you hunh?

Pause.

When
My platoon came back I was
Very focused on
Jonny so I didn't ask about the joint op
I didn't even hear about what happened in the bunker until the locals started
complaining about the smell.

Transition.

End of Part Two.

PART THREE—INTERVIEW WITH PRIVATE JONNY HENDERSON

JONNY *speaks to the journalist. He's holding a cigarette, a lighter. He's wearing the pants from his army uniform as well as a hospital bracelet.*

PTE. JONNY HENDERSON:
This is the first time I've put these pants on in
Uh
Uh
Like five months
It's pretty good
You mind if I smoke?

JONNY *was going to light his smoke but he stops.*

Wow
Forget I asked
Seriously I can't smoke?
Seriously?
Okay fine fuck

JONNY *takes the smoke out of his mouth, fidgets with it.*

My friends
They're all still in Red Deer
They're still working the same jobs they were in high school
One of my buddies he goes to the gym five hours a day
He's on this diet of kidney beans and tuna—his apartment smells like shit
and all he talks about is which protein supplement builds the most muscle
He was like "Don't smoke in my apartment, man" I was like "Seriously, buddy,
it can't smell any worse in here…"

JONNY *laughs or smiles.*

He works at the mall.

JONNY *tries to remember something, then:*

Did you ask me a question?
What was the question?
Oh yeah
Yeah yeah
Uh
The night before the joint op there was a poker game going—I thought about buying in but
But I didn't.

Shift: memory.

JONNY *is standing outside the mess tent at night.*

He's in the dark: the light source is the fluorescents in the mess tent.

There are sounds of sex close by, coming from off stage.

We hear Sergeant HUGHES *talking dirty to* TANYA.

JONNY *puts the smoke back in his mouth and gets out his lighter, but then he gets distracted by the sounds.*

He stands there listening with an unlit cigarette in his mouth.

JONNY *goes to walk away at least once but can't.*

He stands there, listening to HUGHES *and* TANYA, *off stage, through the mess tent wall.*

HUGHES:

Uh yeah. Uh. Yeah do that. Do that. Oh yeah do that.

TANYA:

Do what?

HUGHES:

Uh yeah, *fuck*, you gonna come for me—you gonna come for me?

TANYA:

No?

HUGHES:

Why not? I want you to come, I can't come unless you come: you gonna come for me?

TANYA:

No.

HUGHES:

What'd you mean, "no"?

TANYA:

I can't come yet.

HUGHES:

Are you close?

TANYA:

No.

HUGHES:

I'm close. I'm close—does that feel good—uh, does that feel good to you? What can I do to make you come?

TANYA:
You can *shut up*. Why are you talking like that?

HUGHES:
(*joking*) You want me to shut up for you?

Five to ten seconds of non-word sounds. We hear mostly TANYA.

JONNY *moves as if to walk away, but then he can't. He stands there, cigarette hanging out of his mouth.*

TANYA:
Well don't come yet! Hey! Don't come!

HUGHES:
Oh man, you—okay I'm gonna try not to: don't move. Don't move.

Shift: interview.

It takes Jonny a couple of seconds to shake the memory and talk. He toys with his cigarette.

PTE. JONNY HENDERSON:
Yeah no sorry I uh
I don't like to think about it
(*grinning*) Anyway I thought you were supposed to like win my trust before you ask me that shit?
Yeah we get media training I know all about you fuckers
Look I can't talk to you about the joint op with the Afghan Army 'cause I don't remember it 'cause I
Had my injury
I was in shock
So it's gonna be a short interview 'cause
There's not much I remember so

He shrugs.

Beat.

I don't know
We could talk about the weather
That's been pretty
Shitty
I don't know
It
It wasn't quiet
It's Panjwaii
It wasn't quiet
First day outside the wire
My first op
We lost a guy
We were at KAF for a few weeks waiting to be deployed
We choppered out to the camp
Night flight couldn't fucking see
Unpacked my kit in the dark
Next day
Our first foot patrol
Mahone
He was this
Family guy
Dad-type guy
Talked about his kids a lot
He walked right into the Taliban
I was closest to him
I
Heard AK fire
Ran up
They'd taken his weapon off him he was

Smiles.

Camp got named after him
FOB

Forward Operating Base Mahone
Yeah first day was—

Shift: memory. TANYA *is there.*

It's night, or dusk, and we're somewhere outside at camp, some dark corner.

TANYA *is holding a dead cigarette butt in her hand.*

TANYA:
So? So, buddy? Hell of a first day for you.

JONNY *spits.*

JONNY:
Yuh.

JONNY *spits.*

Ran up. Got the pressure dressing on him. He was... yelling...

Beat.

TANYA:
You okay?

JONNY:
Just—I like can't feel my... anything: is that normal?

TANYA:
You'll come out of that. Then you'll feel *really fucking bad.*

TANYA *flicks her cigarette butt away. Then she sticks a couple of fingers in her mouth, runs them along her gums while she says:*

I just smoked a pack of smokes; I think my gums are bleeding.

JONNY:
You came to like... find me, to see if I'm okay?

TANYA:
Yeah.

Beat.

If we're gonna stand here, buddy, you can distract me at least.

JONNY:
(*sexual, grinning*) How? You mean like... sexy?

He clicks at her.

TANYA:
(*formal, a warning*) Private?

JONNY:
Okay: Sorry, I'm just kidding. Sergeant flipped out. He punched the dirt.
Did you see that?

TANYA:
(*shrugs*) He gets emotional about his guys.

JONNY:
You...? Like the sarge?

TANYA:
(*shrugs*) *I don't know, sure:* I did a tour with him, he's... like family, like a...
older brother—actually he's kinda like my dad.

JONNY:
Yeah?

TANYA:
Yeah, my dad can talk you into doing things like lending him your boyfriend's car that you happen to have the keys to, so he can go crash it into a parked car in Mississauga.

JONNY:
Car was totalled?

TANYA:
That boyfriend was so good about it too—didn't freak out. Just said, "Shit happens."

JONNY:
Nice guy?

TANYA:
Nice guy.

JONNY:
I'm that guy: nice guy.

TANYA:
Yeah?

JONNY:
There was this girl in high school—her name was Sarah Jean Greene—I did stuff like that for her, like when her cat ran away I put up posters for it, for her… cat, and I was always throwing myself off stuff to impress her—

TANYA:
Like what?

JONNY:
I jumped off a portable at school and broke my arm.

They laugh.

Yeah, it sucked.

TANYA:
So?

JONNY:
So?

TANYA:
What happened to her?

JONNY:
She's still in Red Deer? Oh we're not dating now or anything: I'm… single—?

TANYA:
Yeah but what happened, you uh…?

JONNY:
No, no. She wrote on my cast though: "Get better hugs Sarah Jean." But no, I didn't get lucky. She was on the virginity committee at school, actually. That should have uh… clued me in. But I respected that. I could respect that. I mean *I'm* not a virgin! I'm… not a virgin: my first time was on a spin the bottle.

JONNY spits.

Some girl in from Calgary, someone's cousin. She was nineteen, I was fifteen. She kept saying, "You're so cute, you're so cute, Jonny, you're so cute." She had on a T-shirt with the word cute on it: it was up against my face the whole time; I couldn't even see what was happening.

Beat.

TANYA:
You lost your virginity playing spin the bottle.

JONNY:
Yeah.

JONNY spits.

TANYA:
Wow.

JONNY:
Yeah.

TANYA:
So—wow—the bottle's going around and you're fucking *hoping* it's not the fat girl on the field hockey team.

JONNY:
(laughing) Yeah!

TANYA:
I was on the field hockey team.

JONNY:
Yeah?

TANYA:
Goalie.

JONNY:
Hot.

TANYA:
Opposite of hot.

JONNY:
Hot.

TANYA:
I wore a metal bra that was kind of hot.

JONNY kisses TANYA.

After a moment TANYA pulls back.

JONNY immediately says:

JONNY:
Yeah, I'm sorry: sorry I... just kissed you? I don't know why I just did that.
Yeah—I don't know why I did that—I mean I have a thing for you but that
was weird—wrong—I'm sorry.

TANYA:
It's okay.

Beat.

JONNY:
Are you gonna charge me?

TANYA:
No.

Beat.

JONNY:
Can I do it again?

TANYA:
No.

Beat.

JONNY:
(*charming*) But... can I do it again?

Beat. Then low, sincere:

I want to so... bad, like...

TANYA looks at him.

When—and only when—JONNY gets a physical cue from TANYA, he kisses her.

It's sexy. Sexy because JONNY is so infatuated.

TANYA breaks it off.

TANYA:
Yeah—no—this is—no—

JONNY:
Two minutes.

TANYA:
That supposed to convince me?

JONNY:
Five minutes?

Pause. TANYA considers, wavers.

TANYA:
Two minutes.

JONNY smiles, moves back towards her.

Two.

Shift: interview. TANYA *is gone.*

JONNY *is still toying with the cigarette.*

PTE. JONNY HENDERSON:
Shit sorry I
Lost my train of thought there
It's just my
First day out in Panjwaii was uh

He shakes his head.

Mahone?
He knew he was dead
He could see there was a lot of blood
Kept saying "Shit I'm bleeding out"
Then he did
Yeah
First day I hosed blood off my tac vest
Kept dropping the hose
Kept dropping my tac vest
I thought I was fine
I was like "Oh I'm fine I'm fine oh I'm fine"
But I was uh
Uh
Okay can I please smoke this fucking thing now?
Come on seriously?
Why?
You think these things'll kill me?

JONNY *puts the cigarette in his mouth and goes to light it.*

Shift: memory.

TANYA *is fixing her clothes, pulling on one of her boots, etc.* JONNY *is watching her, unlit cigarette dangling from his mouth, trying to light it, but he's fumbling it.*

JONNY:

Shit, I dropped my lighter. I can't—I can't feel my fingers: I can't even smoke this. I think I'm... cold: I hosed all this... blood off my tac vest. I'm all *damp*.

JONNY stops trying to light the cigarette and kisses TANYA. *She stops him after a moment, after he goes to pull her clothes down and have sex with her again.* TANYA *keeps fixing her clothes through the dialogue below.*

TANYA:

No, that's it, buddy—I'm going to the shacks—you?

JONNY:

What: *now?*

TANYA:

Yeah: now.

JONNY:

Yeah? Okay, okay...? No, wait, wait, though: now what?

TANYA:

(*fixing her clothes*) Uhhhhhmm? We... go to sleep, get up, go on patrol, go to sleep, get up, go on patrol, for six months: almost like we're in the army.

JONNY:

Seriously? So I'm supposed to look at you and not touch?

TANYA:

Yeah, it's like a strip club.

TANYA has finished fixing her clothes and goes to exit.

JONNY:

Come on! I—wait—wait! You know I like you? Like...

TANYA:
Like…?

JONNY:
Long term.

Beat. TANYA *looks at* JONNY.

TANYA:
You're twenty years old: how old are you?

JONNY:
Twenty—?

TANYA:
You're twenty. You haven't even—you're from Red Deer, this your first time outside Red Deer—

JONNY:
No—?

TANYA:
My mom just got arrested on a DUI. I grew up in *Hamilton,* you know where that is—?

JONNY:
No? So—?

TANYA:
So nothing.

Beat.

JONNY:
What the fuck are you talking about?!

TANYA:

I'm saying you fucked me standing up. That's a cheap fuck, that's not / "long-term commitment material"—

JONNY:

No, no: come on—come on: why? There are guys like me. I don't want to be single my whole… twenties, what's good about that? There's nothing good about not having you in my life. I wanna commit. Don't *laugh!* There are guys like me who know what they want at twenty—Mahone was twenty-six, he has two kids—

TANYA:

You want two kids with me.

JONNY:

I mean not right away, but…! I'm not saying this well, but I'm like… showing you my heart.

Beat.

(*mumbling*) I think I'm… love you… uh… uh I'm… shaking—I just… hosed all this blood off my tac vest, w… will you just come here for a second…?

JONNY *goes to hold her.*

TANYA *backs up.*

Then wh… why'd you even…? Why'd you even…?

TANYA:

I don't know. Why do I do anything: to distract myself for two minutes?

Beat.

You—okay: it's not like I'm handing it out to just anyone—that gonna hold you?

ANDERS enters from another direction.

Shit, I'm going.

TANYA exits.

JONNY watches her go.

ANDERS sees JONNY standing there.

ANDERS:
Jonny?

JONNY turns.

JONNY:
Uh. Uh. Uh yeah, yeah…

JONNY turns to look behind him, looks back at ANDERS.

ANDERS:
You… staring *at* something, or—?

JONNY:
Uh, y… yeah, nothing—!

ANDERS:
You okay there?

JONNY:
Yeah! Good! Y… yeah!

ANDERS:
You can say no.

JONNY:
I'm good!

Beat.

ANDERS:
I… heard you… got the worst of Mahone today.

JONNY:
Uh…! Yeah!

ANDERS:
Can you look at me for a sec?

JONNY:
Yeah!

JONNY looks at ANDERS.

JONNY is dazed, shaking, in shock.

ANDERS:
Listen, Jonny, I'm going to go keep your sergeant company: come with me.

JONNY:
Nah, I'm good—

ANDERS:
Come keep your sarge company with me.

JONNY:
Nah, nah, I—

ANDERS:
'Cause probably from here you'll go pretty low and… that's gonna suck if that happens when you're back in the shacks by yourself. 'N' then what happens

is I come to your bunk and I play my guitar to cheer you up, and most of the songs I know are from Bible studies camp. You don't want to bring that on yourself, okay?

JONNY:
Nah, I'm good—

ANDERS:
No, I don't think you are.

Beat.

Come on!

Shift: interview.

PTE. JONNY HENDERSON:
Yeah!
Yeah
Sorry I'm with you
I'm still with you
I'm fine that first day was just
Uh
Uh
Busy
I told you why
I just told you why
Mahone
Yeah that's all I've got to say about it next question—

Shift: memory. HUGHES *and* ANDERS *are there.*

JONNY *is sitting with them outside the shacks.*

HUGHES:
(*to* ANDERS) You ever meet Mahone's wife? She's cute as a button. All *blond.* So are the kids. They're two and five. Little boy's five.

Pause. HUGHES *shakes his head, gets pissed off, paces.*

JONNY *and* ANDERS *watch him.* ANDERS *gets up and stops him, gets in his way, gets hold of him by the shoulders.*

ANDERS:
Hey, you're okay. You're okay.

HUGHES:
(*very low, to* ANDERS, *like he can't believe it*) That's one of... *my guys,* they *fucking...?*

ANDERS:
Yeah.

HUGHES:
(*low, to* ANDERS) They took his rifle off him: we don't even see them?

HUGHES *shakes his head.*

HUGHES *walks around* ANDERS, *paces again.* JONNY *and* ANDERS *watch him.*

Two little kids, two and five. I had a barbecue at his house a month ago—I had hot dogs at his house—

ANDERS:
(*gently*) It's not on you.

HUGHES:
It—yeah it is. Who's it / on?

ANDERS:

No, it's not. It's not on you: it's on / them.

HUGHES:

Fucking… Taliban… sneak the fuck up, put their hands on him…?

Beat.

Uhhh we… talked about our kids, in the mess, last night. I said some dumb thing about…!

Beat.

ANDERS:

Yeah.

HUGHES:

Yeah.

There is a pause as HUGHES *tries to pull himself out of it.*

Uh! Uh, *fuck me:* you know what I need? I need *a fucking drink,* and by *drink* I mean…

HUGHES *pretends to hump* ANDERS.

ANDERS:

Hey now!

HUGHES:

Nelson's going on leave; you hear where he's going?

JONNY:

Thailand.

ANDERS:
Hooters.

HUGHES:
Aw, *man!* The no-drinking, no-sex parts of the military are…! Well let's just say they're "not my favourite" parts. *Not my favourite.* My daughter said to me, "I don't like Katy," this one little girl at her kindergarten. I said to her, "Bella, we don't say that. We like everyone. Until they do something bad to us. Then we fuck them up." I didn't say that. Bella says to me, she says: "Can I say Katy is not my favourite?" Cute kid. Looks like her mother.

ANDERS:
How is she?

HUGHES:
My… daughter?

ANDERS:
Your wife.

HUGHES:
We're separated.

ANDERS:
Oh. *What!* I didn't know that! When did that happen?

HUGHES:
It was… end of my last tour.

JONNY:
I'm sorry, man.

ANDERS:
Yeah! I'm… sorry to hear that?

HUGHES:

It happens, right? Now she's with this guy—he sells farming equipment. Combines. Hog feeders. The one thing that pisses me off—he lives in my house, with my wife, and my daughter, and this is what pisses me off—*my dog likes this guy.*

They all laugh or smile.

Follows him around.

ANDERS:

It… happened while you were over here?

HUGHES:

Sure did.

ANDERS:

How'd you… find out?

HUGHES:

Email.

ANDERS:

She emailed you.

HUGHES:

(*grinning, to* ANDERS) On the plus side, Anders, you know what I'd forgot? Girls like me. Nurses. Nurses like me. Halliburton girls—

ANDERS:

That's…! That's *great*—

HUGHES:

(*to* ANDERS) You thought I was still with my wife: you just treated me for chlamydia?

ANDERS:
I... don't ask.

HUGHES:
(*to* JONNY) You been hanging out with any hot girls, Jonny?

JONNY:
Me? You mean... at home?

HUGHES:
At home? At KAF?

ANDERS:
Hey, hey now! You can't ask him that!

(*to* JONNY, *reminding*) Jonny, what you do is your own business. Just... don't get caught and your sarge won't have to send you home for... fraternization, okay?

HUGHES:
(*grinning*) I gotta hunch there's a girl he likes.

JONNY:
There was a... a girl in high school. She was this nice girl: she was a big Christian—

HUGHES:
Anders is a big Christian.

JONNY:
Yeah?

ANDERS:
I'm a Christian, yeah. You're not?

JONNY:
Sure. Just not a big one.

The three of them smile and/or laugh a little bit.

(to ANDERS*)* Like for funerals I'm Christian?

HUGHES:
So no hot girls. No one. You and the master corporal.

JONNY looks at HUGHES. ANDERS looks at HUGHES too.

ANDERS:
(to HUGHES) Drop it.

HUGHES:
(to JONNY) No?

JONNY:
No!

HUGHES:
Sure.

JONNY:
No, it's nothing,

HUGHES:
I see why you like her.

JONNY:
I—no—

HUGHES:
When?

ANDERS:
(to HUGHES) Hey! Drop it! Come on.

HUGHES:

(to ANDERS*)* Well I can't ask you: you're not into girls.

ANDERS *shoots* HUGHES *a look, a pissed-off warning. Meanwhile,* JONNY *laughs, then stops laughing when he realizes that* HUGHES *might mean it.*

JONNY:

(looking between them) Seriously? *Seriously.*

ANDERS:

(to JONNY*)* No.

JONNY:

(to HUGHES*)* Seriously?

HUGHES:

(to JONNY*)* No, no, I'm just fucking with him. So at KAF? Or… here? You're kidding me—here? When? Ten minutes ago?

JONNY:

(smiling) Like I said—

HUGHES:

(to JONNY*)* It was last night? You fit that in—you unpack your kit and you go and—?

JONNY:

It was—no.

HUGHES:

So tonight? Tonight? Last night?

JONNY:

Nah, it—it wasn't last night.

HUGHES *laughs, pats* JONNY *on the back. Meanwhile* ANDERS *is staring at* HUGHES, *pissed off.* HUGHES *clocks this and his apology is half to* ANDERS.

HUGHES:
Sorry! Sorry, buddy, I shouldn't have… made you… tell me that. I just took this course in tactical questioning…

(to ANDERS, *still laughing)* Sorry!

JONNY:
(to HUGHES*)* I guess you could tell I have a thing for her?

HUGHES:
(grinning) Couldn't tell at all.

JONNY:
(to ANDERS*)* You… gonna pray for Mahone?

ANDERS:
Yeah.

Shift: interview. HUGHES *and* ANDERS *are gone.*

JONNY *shakes his head.*

PTE. JONNY HENDERSON:
Yeah
Yeah that
That sounds right it was yeah
First day was
Mahone
Coupl'a patrols out into the villages and then
Yeah
The joint op was a week later
Maybe five days?
Oh you know that for sure it was a week?

Okay
Then yeah
A week after we deployed to the FOB we went on the joint op with the
Afghan Army
(*shrugging*) I mean
Sure
I mean sure I can try to tell but like I said I don't remember it
Sure
Okay
Uh
Sorry shit what was the question again?
The night before the joint op
The night before the joint op I uh
No I didn't play poker I just caught the
The end of the
Game of poker

TANYA *is there, in the mess tent, fixing her clothes, picking up the cards.* JONNY
looks at her for a second, then says to the interviewer:

Yeah that was a bad night
I don't know it was just a bad night
I don't know
'Cause
I'd been kinda holding out
Holding out for this thing it was kinda my

JONNY *looks over at* TANYA *again, picking up cards, for a second, then says to
the interviewer:*

Look no reason
That night was just a bad night.

Shift: memory.

JONNY:
You still playing?

A beat as TANYA *turns and looks at* JONNY *for a split second to try and work out what he knows.*

TANYA:
Game just ended.

JONNY:
Oh yeah? Who won?

TANYA:
I did.

JONNY:
How much?

TANYA:
Seventy bucks. Why are you up: go to sleep—

JONNY:
(holding up a couple of the bent cards) Did you sit on the fucking cards?

TANYA:
Yeah, I rolled around in them after I won. I'm gonna hit the sack—

JONNY:
Yeah?

TANYA:
Yep.

JONNY:
Wanna play a round with me?

Beat.

TANYA:
I just said I'm tired, I'm gonna / hit the sack.

JONNY:
You wanna play a round with me?

TANYA looks at JONNY.

Then JONNY gets hold of TANYA. JONNY is aggressive about it.

TANYA:
Get... off—

JONNY kisses TANYA forcibly, aggressively. TANYA lets him for a few beats. Then she starts trying to push him off her.

Get off / me.

JONNY:
Come on.

TANYA:
Get / off!

JONNY:
Come on: what do you care?

TANYA:
Get the fuck off me, Jonny. Jesus.

TANYA pushes him off of her.

Pause while they look at each other.

Don't do that. Come on, buddy. Don't be that guy.

TANYA *picks up her seventy bucks and goes to exit.*

As she's exiting:

JONNY:
Well don't go…? Don't… go.

TANYA'S *gone.*

(to himself) I was… in the shacks, right over there… if you wanted to just like… fuck someone, you could have come and got me I would have done that for you. I did it a week ago…?

Beat.

Stupid, stupid, stupid, stupid, stupid, stupid, stupid, stupid, *stupid!*

As JONNY *says the last "stupid," he kicks a crate chair over and stamps on it, pissed off. It's loud, we hear the sound of wood splintering.*

Then JONNY *sits down and unslings his C8 rifle and balances it against the floor.* JONNY *rests his forehead against the barrel of the rifle, just rests it there.*

Then JONNY *picks his head up off the rifle and looks down the barrel of it for a second.*

(to himself) Do it, just fucking do it…

ANDERS *enters and sees him there, looking down the barrel.*

JONNY *looks up at* ANDERS.

Then JONNY *shifts the rifle away, puts his head down in his hands.*

ANDERS *stands there.*

What?

ANDERS:
I came in: I heard a bang.

ANDERS *comes over, looks at the wrecked crate chair.*

You pissed off?

JONNY:
I'm fine.

ANDERS *sits down beside* JONNY.

I'm fine!

ANDERS:
You were uh—you were looking down the barrel of your rifle—

JONNY:
Yeah, no, I'm fine, needs a clean.

ANDERS:
Okay if I sit here with you?

JONNY:
Yeah.

ANDERS:
Just saw... Tanya? Looked a lot like you. Well, no, you look worse. You 'n' her, you still uh... fraternizing—you don't have to tell me.

JONNY:
No, I'm just...

Beat.

ANDERS:
(*sharp*) Jonny!

JONNY:
What!

ANDERS:
Look at me for a sec.

Beat. JONNY looks at him, looks him straight in the eyes. No problem, but he's hostile.

Is this about... Mahone, because you know that his injury—you know it was his... artery: what happened was going to happen no matter what you did—is there something he said to you or you... saw that you're reliving... seeing again and again?

JONNY:
Yeah: no—

ANDERS:
If you're starting to feel... numbed out or... agitated—

JONNY:
Yeah! No, it's not Mahone.

ANDERS:
Hey, hey, it happens. Guys can get a little numbed out, especially when there's been a / lot going on—

JONNY:
It's—yeah— / No.

ANDERS takes JONNY's rifle away from him.

ANDERS:
Yeah, I'm gonna send you back to KAF for a bit, get you some rest—

JONNY:
What—no.

ANDERS:
Hey: I'm just saying "some / rest."

JONNY:
No, come / on—

ANDERS:
You can catch a ride out with resup—

JONNY:
Come on, it's just... Tanya! It's nothing! Just... girls suck, I'm fine, just a bad night.

Beat.

Just—nothing—it was nothing—just a bad night, I got pissed off: I was... fucking around with my r... rifle.

Beat.

ANDERS:
Yeah?

JONNY:
Yeah, it's nothing: it's just... *embarrassing*—don't look at me like that, man, seriously, it's nothing.

Beat.

ANDERS:
(smiling) Girls suck?

JONNY:
Yeah, they do! And it's shitty 'cause...

Beat.

ANDERS:
(trying not to smile now) 'Cause you... like her a lot.

JONNY:
You know what? I'm just gonna play the asshole card from now on, man. Fuck it: at least I... fucked her. Fuck it—

ANDERS:
Okay, can you—you think you'll be able to shrug it off—?

JONNY:
Yeah yeah.

Beat. ANDERS *looks at him.*

Yeah?

ANDERS *hands* JONNY *his rifle back.*

ANDERS:
Okay. You're okay. You're okay. I'm uh—I'll just sit here with you, for a little, if that's okay?

Beat.

JONNY:
I wrecked that thing.

ANDERS:
(*testing it out, wobbling it, smiling*) Yeah! Yeah, I think you did!

JONNY:
Sorry.

Shift: interview. ANDERS *is gone.*

PTE. JONNY HENDERSON:
Sorry
Sorry aw man I'm really wandering what was the question?
Okay yeah
Yeah the joint op with the Afghan Army 'n' right away it went bad
There was this
Holdup

Shift: memory. We're back on sentry at camp.

JONNY *sees* TANYA *there. He's distracted by her.*

This situation with
With uh

Pause as JONNY *looks at* TANYA *again, then:*

JONNY:
Hey, that terp? He asked me if it's true you're a woman. He should've been outside the mess tent last night, I think that would've... uh...

TANYA *has turned and is looking at* JONNY.

He clicks at her.

Beat.

Then he asked me if you fuck all of us or just him.

TANYA *punches* JONNY *in the head. He goes down hard, on his ass.* HUGHES *enters, running, and gets between them, gets hold of* TANYA.

Simultaneously:

HUGHES:
(to TANYA*)* Hey! Hey!!!

TANYA:
(to JONNY*)* Don't *touch* me!

JONNY:
I didn't touch you!

HUGHES:
Hey! / Hey, hey!

TANYA:
(to JONNY*, fully losing her shit)* Hey fuck you, you shitty little kid, go fuck yourself—

HUGHES:
HEY / HEY—!

TANYA:
—little cherry bitch, fucking prairie boy—

HUGHES:
HEY!

TANYA:
I'm gonna *fucking kill you.*

HUGHES *pulls* TANYA *away from* JONNY. *He stands between* JONNY *and* TANYA, *blocks* TANYA's *view of* JONNY. JONNY *touches his face, sitting on the ground. We start to hear a faint ringing sound.*

HUGHES:

(*to* TANYA) Hey! No, look at me. What's going on? Master Corporal?

TANYA is furious, panting. She shakes her head at HUGHES.

Okay, go for a walk. Go for a / walk.

TANYA:

Yeah, I'm…! I'm going for a walk.

TANYA exits.

JONNY is still staring after TANYA, never takes his eyes off her.

The ringing sound is louder now.

HUGHES kneels down beside JONNY, looks at his face.

HUGHES:

How's your face? She got you good. What was that?

Beat.

What was that?

Beat.

You gonna cry?

JONNY shrugs HUGHES off of him and stumbles up.

The ringing sound is even louder now.

Shift: interview.

PTE. JONNY HENDERSON:
No nothing

Beat.

Nothing
It was
Nothing it was just a holdup just a little local kid with his guts spilling out
he needed a medic
Yeah nothing just one of the worst uh

Beat.

We
Get out there to this village
For a while there we were taking a lot of fire
We were in
Serious shit my uh
Weapon the barrel was glowing that's how much I fired it
I heard this
Snap
It was a bullet took a chunk out of the ditch
Right beside my arm in the ditch
It was
Tense
And then uh
Then

Beat.

Then the Taliban retreat back into the compound 'n' we're waiting in the
ditch for orders
It was us and the Afghan Army
'N' we're all tweaked—I mean we're all laughing 'cause the contact was so
Tense
Then

This villager in a
Burka
Walked up along the road she's got a little
Toddler by the hand
I
Yelled to her
Go back
Go back
She saw me
She picked up her kid turned around and ran
Couple of minutes later there's this boy on a bike
He was
I don't know
Fifteen
Sixteen
He was riding up to the ditch on his
Bike
Bicycle
So I yell
Get back
I don't know
Ten
Twenty times
Get back
Get the fuck back
And I don't know
I mean I don't know
Maybe he's tweaked from the firefight
Maybe he's deaf
The fuck do I know?
O'Hare's turning around
He's yelling
Yelling something
Take him out?
I'm looking at this kid

Beat.

I see his face

Pause. JONNY *sees the boy's face.*

And that's it
That's all I remember
Took a couple of teeth and cut into my lips and gums
My chest was worst hit
My stomach
My
Uh
Uh
My
I know in the chopper I stopped breathing

He smiles.

Most of it got fixed
Not
Not all of it

Beat. He takes a breath.

O'Hare had a lot of
It was his neck
Like an inch from clipping his
Neck

Beat.

So that

Beat.

I don't know why I didn't fire
That's the
That's the
Yeah
Try not to
I don't know the kid was a
Kid
I don't know I was off my game that day

Beat. JONNY *shakes it off.*

I'm gonna be in hospital for a while
I'm gonna be here in Calgary for a while
For my family
For Mom and Dad I have to
Be strong about it
N'uh
Get better
Get as much better as I can
Yeah
Yeah still in hospital yeah
'Cause of
My bladder was pretty ripped up
And uh
Stuff
All that stuff got

JONNY *gestures.*

They keep telling me I have to think of it like this is normal now
This is my normal

Beat. JONNY *smiles.*

So like I said I don't know what happened on the joint op that's the closest I got
I was there but I didn't get any closer than the ditch.

JONNY smiles.

Transition.

End of Part Three.

PART FOUR—INTERVIEW WITH SERGEANT STEPHEN HUGHES

HUGHES *speaks to the interviewer.*

SGT. STEPHEN HUGHES:
Listen
We're trying to stabilize that country
We were there to provide security
Get those people some human
Rights—why's that funny
No
Why's that funny
We were trying to help those people
What're you doing with your life that anyone's going to remember in forty-five minutes?

Beat.

The night before the joint op?

He grins.

Why do you give a shit about the night before the joint op?
You just
Trying to get me talking?

He grins. Then, very deliberately:

The
Night before the op I
Couldn't fucking sit still
I played a little poker to try and blow off some steam.

Shift: memory.

HUGHES is exiting the mess tent. He has a slight limp as he exits.

JONNY is standing outside.

There's an unlit cigarette dangling from JONNY's lips.

HUGHES:
(over his shoulder, to TANYA) Don't forget your seventy bucks.

Beat. HUGHES sees JONNY.

Private. Just lost five bucks. Tanya cleaned up. She's in there counting her money. You good?

JONNY looks at him.

You okay?

JONNY looks at him.

You gonna smoke that? You okay?

JONNY takes the cigarette out of his mouth and moves as if to go into the tent. HUGHES stops him, puts a hand on his shoulder.

Hey, hey, no: let's just—might want to… give her a sec in there.

HUGHES pats JONNY on the back.

You good, Private? You okay? You look a little…?

JONNY walks past him into the tent. As he walks past:

(calling after him) Jonny, I just said d…

Pause. HUGHES *hesitates, considers for a second, clicks at himself, and then turns away from the mess tent.*

Shift: interview.

SGT. STEPHEN HUGHES:
I shouldn't have been playing poker that night it was stupid
I
I uh lost
(*grins*) I lost that game.

HUGHES:
(*turning into the scene*) ANDERS!!!

ANDERS *is there: he reacts immediately to* HUGHES's *yell.*

ANDERS:
Uh!

Shift: memory.

It is nighttime: dark and hard to see. We're at camp, a few steps away from the mess tent towards the shacks. There's some glow coming from the mess tent fluorescents. HUGHES *is still limping slightly.*

Uh! Uh I didn't see you / there!

HUGHES:
(*giggling*) Sorry! Sorry—

ANDERS:
Uh, man...!

ANDERS *is bent almost double.*

HUGHES:
(*giggling*) I stain your pants for you, buddy? Coupl'a drops…?

ANDERS:
Uh…! *What was that?*

HUGHES:
(*giggling*) Sorry, I don't know: I was just playing some… poker. I'm sorry, buddy, I love you—

ANDERS:
I'm gonna have a twitch tomorrow; you scared the… *crap* out of me!

ANDERS *stands back up and* HUGHES *half-hugs him or hangs off of him, leans against him, rests his forehead against him.*

HUGHES:
Anders, you're soft.

ANDERS:
Yeah, screw you.

Pause.

HUGHES:
(*regret, groaning*) Uhhhh!

ANDERS:
What is it, buddy?

HUGHES:
I feel sick.

ANDERS:
Why…?

HUGHES:
Mm, I'm an animal.

ANDERS:
Well, yeah.

HUGHES:
The fuck's wrong with me, Anders? The fuck are you when I get all *tweaked*, buddy? Uhhhh, I have a stomach ache: pit of my stomach…!

ANDERS:
Yeah? Why? You're thinking on… tomorrow, or what?

HUGHES *has his arms, loosely, around* ANDERS's *shoulders by now.*

HUGHES:
(*giggling*) I'm thinking—you know what I'm thinking? We shouldn't let women in the military: what would you do if I just… punched you right now? Just to feel better…?

HUGHES *and* ANDERS *are both giggling by now, a little uncontrollably. They spar with each other during the below dialogue.*

What are *you* doing! You just… walking around in the dark?

ANDERS:
It's a little… adrenalized, in the shacks, just… they're tweaked about tomorrow. There's been some… vomiting… happening. I needed some air. You okay there?

HUGHES:
Uhhhhhh…

ANDERS:
(*gently*) What happened: you're tweaked, buddy? You thinking on… how you're going to keep these guys alive tomorrow?

HUGHES:
(*nods, then moaning from regret*) Uhhhhhhh, make it better, Anders.

ANDERS:
(*gently, smiling*) Why? Something... happen? What happened? What'd you do?

Beat.

HUGHES:
Hey, can I ask you: you uh... still with your uh—with your uh... uh... uh guy?

Beat.

You still with your guy—?

ANDERS:
Yeah.

HUGHES:
Good! Good! Is it just... no—just no... hassles?

Beat.

ANDERS:
Uh. Uh—

HUGHES:
Nothing, nothing: I don't know what I'm talking about—but uh... can you... humour me on something?

ANDERS:
Uh...? What—what... are you...? What are you... thinking you're... gonna *do?* You... gonna punch me, or... y...?

HUGHES:

I fucking want to just… *feel better.* (*charming*) Wait. What are you saying: *can I?!*

ANDERS:

Can you… what?

Beat.

HUGHES:

(*charming, intimate*) Can I?

ANDERS:

Uh yeah.

Beat.

So do it.

Pause. The men are standing together, very close, very intimate, looking at each other. It's the precipice, a suspended moment: it could tip either way. ANDERS *goes to kiss* HUGHES *and then* HUGHES *backs up a step and/or looks away and says, more formally:*

HUGHES:

Can you humour me, buddy, can you… go into the mess tent, make sure it's… okay?

Beat.

ANDERS:

Yeah…? Go into the mess tent, okay? Okay. What am I going to find in there…?

HUGHES:

Probably nothing.

ANDERS:
Okay…?

Shift: interview.

SGT. STEPHEN HUGHES:
Then I went over the orders
Yeah
Yeah Zaeef
Yeah the Afghan National Army commander that's Zaeef
Yeah he's used colourful tactics in the past
So have the Taliban but I planned to hold his hand the whole way
Look
We want to go home
They want us to go home
That means we co-operate with Afghan authorities in this case the ANA so
there's someone to hand the country back over to
That is
Other than the Taliban
Take your fucking pick

Beat.

Day of the joint op
I had this one thing running in my head
This uh
This one thing always runs in my head
I want to do right by my guys
I'm responsible for them
For their lives
That's on me
That's the main thing I want to do right by them.

Shift: memory.

TANYA *punches* JONNY *in the head. He goes down hard, on his ass.* HUGHES *enters, running, and gets between them, gets hold of* TANYA.

Simultaneously:

HUGHES:
(to TANYA*)* Hey! Hey!!!

TANYA:
(to JONNY*)* Don't *touch* me!

JONNY:
I didn't touch you!

HUGHES:
Hey! / Hey, hey!

TANYA:
(to JONNY, *fully losing her shit)* Hey *fuck you, you shitty little kid,* go fuck yourself—

HUGHES:
HEY / HEY—!

TANYA:
—little cherry bitch, fucking prairie boy—

HUGHES:
HEY!

TANYA:
I'm gonna *fucking kill you.*

HUGHES *pulls* TANYA *away from* JONNY. *He stands between* JONNY *and* TANYA, *blocks* TANYA's *view of* JONNY. JONNY *touches his face and stares up at* TANYA.

HUGHES:
(*to* TANYA) Hey! No, look at me. What's going on? Master Corporal?

TANYA is furious, panting. She shakes her head at HUGHES.

Okay, go for a walk. Go for a / walk.

TANYA:
Yeah, I'm...! I'm going for a walk.

TANYA exits.

HUGHES kneels down beside JONNY, looks at his face.

HUGHES:
How's your face? She got you good. What was that?

Beat.

What was that?

Beat.

You gonna cry?

JONNY shrugs HUGHES off of him and stumbles up.

What's going on?

JONNY:
I don't know.

HUGHES:
You say something to her? What'd you say?

JONNY:
What d'you think I said?

Beat.

HUGHES:
Okay, okay: I didn't think it—okay, it was a big thing to you?

JONNY:
(*hostile*) Sergeant.

HUGHES:
Okay, buddy, you're *twenty*, you... Really? You have it that bad for her?

JONNY:
(*hostile*) Sergeant.

HUGHES shakes his head, looks at JONNY. JONNY looks back at him, totally blank, unblinking, pissed off.

HUGHES:
Okay, yeah, *shit*, I'm sorry. I'm sorry: it's my bad. Listen, I wasn't trying to... take your girlfriend: I was just... being a fucking idiot and I—if I thought you... didn't want me to, I wouldn't have done it. I'm sorry, Jonny. We good?

Beat.

We good?

JONNY shakes his head, touches his jaw.

JONNY:
(*hostile*) My ears are... ringing; I can like... barely hear you?

JONNY crouches down, touches his ear.

HUGHES:
(to himself) Fuck.

Shift: interview.

SGT. STEPHEN HUGHES:
The combat we saw that day was the most effective resistance we'd met with
so far in Panjwaii
First of all one of the things we rely on is the Taliban don't know how to fire
their weapons
I don't know why
They think weapons fire themselves
On the joint op
The Taliban were not only firing accurately but they had a couple of snipers
with them
Nearly fifty-degree heat
Low on water
Low on ammo
No air support
We're taking massive contact from an unknown number of enemy combatants
Then there was the suicide bomber

Shakes his head.

Worst thing is there's so much guts from the kid who's just blown himself up
you don't even know how badly your own soldier's been hit
It was
Yeah
A mess.

Shift: memory. JONNY *is there.*

JONNY *is on the ground.*

His tac vest is bloody.

He has a fentanyl lollipop in his mouth.

HUGHES *is moving towards* JONNY, *calling to his men.*

HUGHES:
Hey. Where's the chopper? What are we waiting on?

(to JONNY*)* Jonny, open your eyes: you have to keep them open—can you see me?

JONNY:
Yeah.

HUGHES:
You have to keep them open.

JONNY *tries to sit up.*

No, don't look—don't look. Keep your eyes on me—

JONNY:
Why?

HUGHES:
We're just waiting on the chopper: Can you tell me what day of the week it is?

JONNY:
I don't fucking know—do you?

HUGHES:
(laughing: relieved) Hey now. Don't be a smartass.

JONNY:
Where's O'Hare?

HUGHES:

He's fine. He's got a couple of cuts, that's / it.

JONNY:

Where's O'Hare?

HUGHES:

He's fine, he's fine: he's sitting up—he's giving you the finger.

JONNY:

He's dead?

HUGHES:

No, he's fine, it's not your fault.

JONNY is trying to sit up again.

Hey, don't move—

JONNY:

I can't— / I'm uh… dizzy—

JONNY's trying to sit up again.

HUGHES:

I gotcha—I gotcha, it's okay, you're okay, just keep your eyes on me: we're waiting on the chopper—

JONNY:

Where's Tanya?

HUGHES:

She's back at Mahone.

JONNY:

Can you get her… for me—?

HUGHES:

She's back at Mahone.

JONNY:

Where?

HUGHES:

She didn't come, she stayed back, remember?

(calling to his men) Hey! Where's the chopper! What's the update?!

JONNY:

What's wrong with my voice? Do I have a cold?

HUGHES:

You're just missing a couple of teeth: you're going to look like a hockey player. The chicks love that—

JONNY:

Yeah, you think Tanya'll love that—

HUGHES:

Yeah, I do.

JONNY:

Tell her something from me.

HUGHES:

Like what?

JONNY:

I don't know…

HUGHES:

Hey. Hey, Jonny. What should I tell her? *Jonny,* what should I tell her: you want me to tell her you love her?

JONNY:
I love her.

HUGHES:
I know, buddy.

JONNY:
She th… thinks I'm a bad person…

HUGHES:
No she doesn't.

JONNY:
I'm bleeding out, I think…?

HUGHES:
No you're not—don't look.

JONNY:
Yuh…

HUGHES stands.

HUGHES:
(calling to his men) Okay, who the fuck's on comms? Is that Zaeef? No, get off comms. Where the fuck's the chopper—I'm going to *fucking rape them*: where the fuck are they? NO, WHERE THE FUCK ARE THEY! GET ON WITH ZERO AND TELL THEM I'M GONNA *FUCKING RAPE THEM DEAD.* WHERE THE FUCK ARE THEY? *I HAVE A GUY DOWN. WHAT ARE YOU DOING? GET OFF WITH ZAEEF AND GET ON WITH*—AW FUCK, GIVE ME THAT!

Interspersed simultaneously with HUGHES's dialogue above:

JONNY:
I'm… Am I bleeding out? Am I… I'm bleeding out… I'm uh… dizzy… uh…

Shift: interview.

SGT. STEPHEN HUGHES:
We had two soldiers down
We're waiting on the chopper to extract them
Chopper's taking its time
I've lost guys before and we all
We all have feelings

Beat.

Zaeef's on comms
He's saying
"Let's move in there"
It's a joint op
We can't
We have a man down
There's no fucking way I'm going to move until the chopper's extracted my guys
I said: "Go ahead you assault the compound
We'll secure the perimeter"

Beat.

I don't know
I don't know
It's his fucking country
I'm supposed to what
Get on comms
Brief him on the Geneva Convention?

HUGHES *shakes his head.*

Zaeef assaulted the compound
Fought the Taliban down into this
It was a

A mud tunnel
Like a bunker
Zaeef didn't want to follow the Taliban into it
He's not stupid
And what?
Let them bomb the shit out of him at close quarters?
So he
He
Blocked the exit it was this
Hole in the ground
Blocked that then he
Pumped water
Diverted a
He pumped water into the bunker
He could only pump the water in so fast
From what he told us it took about an hour for all the Taliban to drown

Shift: memory.

The lighting shift is phased in, minimal, for this scene.

We hear the sound, less faint now, closer.

Perhaps, cut with the sound from the bunker, is the sound of a Black Hawk MEDEVAC *and small-arms fire.*

There is an extended silence while HUGHES *listens to it.*

He shifts a little, uncomfortably.

Then he shakes it off.

Shift: interview.

Sure yeah I heard
Yelling

I heard yelling
You hear that in combat
No I didn't know what it was
No I didn't know
No I didn't know
No I don't sleep at night—the Taliban rig bombs to children I still see that shit all the time
I'm going to go home to my crappy apartment and see that shit
And you know what?

Pause as HUGHES *fights to stop himself from talking about the incident some more.*

HUGHES *takes a moment to recover.*

Then, very calmly:

Listen
Zaeef's tactics

He shakes his head.

I don't like it either
That's not the kind of combat I like
It's disgraceful
But
On the plus side
We saw heavy fire and there were only two injuries to my guys the day of the joint op

Beat. HUGHES *recovers some more.*

(*grinning*) Three if you count my knee
I blew out my knee—

Shift: memory. ANDERS *is there.*

ANDERS is kneeling down, examining HUGHES's knee.

They're either in or just outside the medical tent back at the FOB.

ANDERS:
Yeah, you've blown out the tendons. Or strained them. You'd need a physiotherapist to tell you which. This hurt?

HUGHES:
Yeah.

ANDERS:
This hurt?

HUGHES:
Yeah.

ANDERS:
Yeah, it's swollen.

HUGHES:
Let me walk around on it for a few days see if that fixes it.

ANDERS:
That won't fix it.

HUGHES:
Might fix it.

ANDERS:
If you, say, caught chlamydia from a Halliburton girl at KAF and you kept having intercourse with her, that wouldn't cure your chlamydia.

HUGHES:
Intercourse? What's intercourse?

ANDERS:
It's how you catch chlamydia.

Beat.

I... called into Role 3: Jonny's still in surgery. They're saying it's his *genitals;* that kid is *twenty years old.* How're you taking that? 'Cause I'm not taking that very well.

HUGHES:
Yeah?

ANDERS:
Yeah, I'm not taking it well *at all*—did he—did he—was he...?

Beat.

HUGHES:
What?

ANDERS:
I think Jonny was—I went into the mess, last night, and...?

(*to* HUGHES) 'Cause I don't think he should have been in combat. I think he probably—am I right? He was being stupid out there—?

HUGHES:
A Taliban blew himself up.

ANDERS:
Yeah?

HUGHES:
Yuh.

ANDERS:
Yeah. No, I think he was uh—I think I screwed that one.

HUGHES:
No, buddy.

ANDERS:
Yeah—no, I did: I *fucked* that. I fucked that one, and I'm not sure I know exactly *why* I fucked that one: *What the fuck happened last night?* You send me into the mess, I'm trying to clean that up for you and I fuck that up with Jonny and now I have to ask myself *why* I made the wrong call…!

TANYA enters.

ANDERS and HUGHES shift, look at her.

TANYA:
(to ANDERS) I… came to ask if… you'd heard anything about Jonny?

ANDERS:
He's still in surgery.

TANYA:
Yeah?

Beat.

ANDERS:
(to both of them) So hey, what happened last night? What the fuck happened last night with Jonny, you guys? 'Cause the two of you look like fucking zombies. I went in the mess last night after I-don't-know-what happened and Jonny was all fucked up, and I could've… called it and sent him back to KAF—!

TANYA:
(to ANDERS) Yeah / that's not—

HUGHES:
(*to* ANDERS) That's not on you.

ANDERS:
Why? Why?

HUGHES:
It's not.

ANDERS:
Why? You think it's on... *you guys?*

HUGHES:
Yeah.

Pause.

ANDERS:
(*to* HUGHES) You... take it to the enemy?

HUGHES:
Yuh.

ANDERS:
Well good. *Fuck them.*

TANYA *gets up and exits.*

Pause.

That civilian casualty that Tanya fired on, that little five-year-old girl she fired on, our last tour: who died? Tanya has a stress injury from that, and it's making her behave out of control, and I think you know that, so if you fucked her last night to make yourself feel better, then that's low of you.

Silence. ANDERS *and* HUGHES *stare off at nothing.*

Okay what? What? You're... still sitting here—what?

Beat.

HUGHES:
I fell through ice... one time, ran across the... canal in uh Ottawa, in...
April—when would I have gone into shock?

ANDERS:
Probably right away.

HUGHES:
Hunh. Hunh. That's if the water's cold?

ANDERS:
Yeah?

HUGHES:
And if the water's not cold?

ANDERS:
You wouldn't go into shock, no.

Beat.

HUGHES:
Yeah, it didn't sound like they...

ANDERS *turns and stares at* HUGHES.

There is a beat as HUGHES *focuses on* ANDERS.

I uh got cornered—I—yeah.

ANDERS:
You—what? You ran across a canal in April: fell through ice?

HUGHES:
Yeah! I… I got a little mm… pissed off, cornered, and I did something stupid: I wanted to get Jonny out of there, and I didn't care what Zaeef was going to do. I knew it would be bad news and guess what?

ANDERS:
(*interrupting*) This was when you had guys injured.

Beat.

HUGHES:
Yeah.

ANDERS:
So you made a call, you had guys injured: you made a call?

HUGHES:
(*low*) Yeah.

ANDERS:
(*as in "so what's the problem"*) So?

Pause.

You… shouldn't be telling me this, am I right?

Beat as HUGHES *turns and meets* ANDERS's *eyes. Then the two men look at each other for a beat.*

Lemme know if your knee gets worse.

Shift: interview. ANDERS *is gone.*

HUGHES *looks at the audience/interviewer.*

SGT. STEPHEN HUGHES:
Hey
This is war.

Transition.

End of Part Four.

PART FIVE—CLEANUP

ANDERS is in a box of light, like the other soldiers were at the top of the play.

He speaks to the interviewer.

SGT. CHRIS ANDERS:
Yeah
I took part in the cleanup
The villagers notified local authorities that there were a large number of
unburied human remains in close proximity to their village
There's a risk of cholera
By the time we got the order to go into the bunker most of the remains had
putrefied
We were hitting fifty degrees Celsius over there so

Beat.

It was hard to tell their ages
But yeah
There were a couple of smaller remains at the bottom of the piles

Beat.

Yeah
They were in piles

Beat.

There were bullet holes in the tunnel near the hole that was the exit so some
of them tried to shoot their way out
But no

Not all of them were armed

Beat.

The
Yeah "smaller remains"
That means adolescent enemy combatants
It was hard to tell
Thirteen
Fourteen

Beat.

The total?
One hundred and sixty-three

Pause. He shrugs.

Maybe they're in heaven

Beat. Then straight to the interviewer:

I think they're in hell—we done?

ANDERS *stands and waits for the next question. The interview light box stays up for five seconds or so.*

Dead silence.

Then the light box snaps out.

End of Part Five.

End play.

INTERVIEW WITH THE PLAYWRIGHT

As part of this series of plays commissioned by The Banff Centre, we asked each playwright to sit down with another contemporary Canadian playwright for a conversation about their writing lives and the plays that came out of the Centre. Hannah Moscovitch was interviewed in May 2013 by Anusree Roy, a Dora Award–winning playwright and actor from Toronto who is best known for her plays Pyaasa, Letters To My Grandma, *and* Brothel #9.

ANUSREE ROY: One of the things that Banff wanted me to ask was about your experience being at The Banff Centre. How has it informed the process of your writing to go from complete isolation to public presentation?

HANNAH MOSCOVITCH: Well it accelerated the process of writing for sure because I had blocks of time where I could be very quiet and alone, and I could try very hard and for a long period to work out what the play would be. That happened in Banff because I had a bunch of consecutive weeks there over two consecutive years. I had a month each year and two weeks of Leighton Studio and then two weeks of playwrights' colony each year. I had the acting colony there too—the acting company—they were able to read the play. I use those resources a lot when I have them, and I like workshops. I find they help me, and they work as a good deadline.

AR: In regards to your own play versus others, are there any plays recently that you've read or seen that you feel resonate with you in some way?

HM: Geez, well I read and see a lot of plays... lots of them resonate!

AR: Recently?

HM: Of course, it all goes out of your head. But I just read *Circle Mirror Transformation* by Annie Baker, an American playwright, and enjoyed that a lot. I've recently been reading a bunch of the young female American playwrights like Amy Herzog and Annie Baker and Sarah Ruhl, sort of our American contemporaries, so I've been interested for some reason in catching up on what they're doing.

AR: And what are you finding in their work that's different from our female Canadian writers?

HM: They are more well-made plays, and I know that can be used pejoratively—and I don't use it that way—but it does feel as though you can... it's got a little bit more... It's like the opposite of reading British work, or European work. The Americans are a little bit more jazzified. They go for big, full endings. Non-ironic endings. It's heavily screen-influenced, I would say. It feels really narrative, like a play that's set in one location with three characters who all—dark secrets of the past emerge over the course of the play. Like a play-play that you can feel will make the audience engage. And there's a little bit less narrative experimentation.

AR: Would say we do that a lot more here?

HM: You know, I would say we're in some sort of medial zone between the Americans and the Europeans and the British. We're somewhere in the middle, so we want that, we want some of that, a little bit of formal or aesthetic experimentation, but we don't want it like the Brits do. *(laughter)*

AR: I wonder why that is, though. I've often wondered that. When I read plays, or when I go to see plays in India, the really good ones, I'm often stunned by the ferociousness that I'm watching on stage. Then when I come back home here, that's when I wonder, "What's happening?" There's sometimes—I will not say always—a bit of a safety net here that I don't find back home in India. With some of the theatres I'm like, "What are you people doing? What's happening?" It's so alive, so political.

HM: It's helpful to try and get a little bit of context for the work that we're making. But that's so interesting, because you experiment with form, for sure. I often think, "Oh, Anusree's like me in this way." You want to do some plays that are set in one location, full-out narrative plays that take you on the character journey. And then you have other pieces where you break down narrative a little bit more and you play all the characters, you ask the audience to engage with their imagination in that way. So I sometimes think that that's very Canadian of us that we're willing to try a range of different ways to communicate story. Whereas you'll see the British commit to an extreme formal experimentation and that will be their whole career and they will write play after play after play like that. So I always notice that Canadians have some weird versatility.

AR: I haven't watched a lot of British plays or read much, but—

HM: I haven't read a lot of Indian plays or read much! My ignorance about that is interesting.

AR: Well, you know, I find its accessibility here a bit more difficult. What I'll ask you, though, is, do you believe in inspiration or do you believe in discipline when writing?

HM: Oh, wow, that's a good question. Do you mean in terms of how I structure my day?

AR: Yeah. Do you say, "I am Hannah Moscovitch, I have X number of commissions, this is the week that I'm working on this," and you write every single day. Or do you say, "I'm going to take a walk and see what inspires me until I'm moved to write."

HM: For sure the former. For sure. I'm self-disciplined, I'm about that. I'm not sure if in the end it produces any better work than it would if I was more interested in inspiration because then all that happens is instead of walking and working it out, you're probably just sitting there grinding through this sometimes horrific personal resistance to sitting there and being stuck and not knowing. Then the abyss opens up beneath you of, "Oh, I'm bad at this," and then you're forced to confront that and move through it.

AR: But it is in that discipline, where you wake up in the morning and you go. Is it just a form of habit from a certain time onwards, or do you go by pages?

HM: I do time. Because I feel like I can't control pages. And I can control time.

AR: So do I. I go from one o'clock to four o'clock or whatever. How long—is there a specific time?

HM: Yeah, I had a schedule kind of pinned to my wall, and of course I broke it constantly, really. But I always wrote ten to four and then I had other things I did the rest of the time, but it was really scheduled. Because writing is so mysterious and inspiration-based sometimes you want to get hold of it and write out a schedule. Or that's my experience of it.

AR: Ten to four. That's a good chunk of time. Do you actually sit in front of the computer that entire time?

HM: I tried. I would, you know, eat lunch. But I had a big thing about putting my pants on in the morning. If you're me, you have to put your pants on.

AR: Meaning you actually dress for work? Every day?

HM: Yeah, I have to or I won't work. I'll just press "play all" on a DVD of *The Sopranos*.

AR: Do you have *The Sopranos* on in the background while you're writing?

HM: When I'm writing, sometimes, if I've gotten really stuck. I have all sorts of tricks.

AR: Like what?

HM: Like tinkering-with-my-own-brain tricks. Sometimes I'll watch TV in the background. The reason for that is it actually alters your brainwaves so it can click you out of—I'll sometimes drink.

AR: While you're writing?

HM: Yeah. Usually not at ten a.m. It's usually desperate measures. That's like a defeat trick. I'm defeated and think, "I'm gonna drink," and sit down and work with a glass of—

AR: Wine?

HM: Vodka, usually. Vodka soda. Pound those back! So I do that. My other tricks are even uglier. They go downhill.

AR: Which is what? I'm sensing medication.

HM: Yeah! *(laughter)*

AR: Percocet?

HM: Yeah. Percocet or Ativan. It's usually—I'm making myself sound like an addict, but obviously you know because you guessed right away.

AR: We talked about this earlier is why I'm guessing.

HM: Well those are good tricks. Usually it's at the beginning of a project when I'm just facing the demons of there being nothing. And sometimes it's better than going through what is more or less a slow-burn panic attack at the beginning of a project.

AR: Have you ever had that? Have you ever had a moment where you sat in front of the computer thinking, "I'm actually panicking right now. I'm having anxiety right now"?

HM: Mm-huh. Yeah, very big, very extreme versions of that, actually. But usually in a moment where I realize that everything is wrong. Or I'll have a moment where I realize that half this play, like fully half of it, needs to be entirely rewritten. It's actually the time that the rewrite is going to take that sends me into the panic.

AR: Yes, because you would just think, "I have fifteen other commissions."

HM: When you have a schedule, like a spreadsheet of when you're going to work on which thing—and you can see that going out—you can start to panic because you know that if it's the right thing you have to pursue it. Usually that sends me into panic. And then losing perspective, that's the other thing.

AR: In what way do you mean?

HM: When I can't tell any more which draft is better, when I can't tell any more if I've made good changes or bad changes.

AR: Yes, I've had that where you think, "Did I just ruin the entire play?" Or, if I'm making this decision, is this the best decision ever. I don't know. Should she stay or should she go was my biggest decision with *Brothel #9*. Is she staying, is she going? What is she doing? Right in the end. Am I making her leave or is she staying? Which one is right? And you're thinking, "I've written it for four years, I actually have no idea."

HM: Endings are hard.

AR: Really, really hard. But speaking of the writing, are there specific rituals that you do as a writer?

HM: I will do really stupid small rewrites on stuff to kind of go in the shallow end. I'll usually allow myself an hour of that just so that I'll get myself on a roll because I'm sort of looking for that mystical (not really mystical) moment where all of my resistance bleeds out of me and I'm just writing and I'm neutral and I'm working. That usually takes a certain amount of time for me to inch my way and convince myself it's going to be okay. So it's usually about an hour that I allow myself to do rewrites—

AR: On other projects?

HM: On that project.

AR: And are there times where you read the entire play all over again just in order to begin the next process?

HM: Yeah. I find that hugely painful sometimes.

AR: So do I! Like an hour and a half goes away just rereading.

HM: And, stupidly, I think I tend to only classify writing as writing—typing as writing—and the thinking I don't classify as writing.

AR: Oh, as time?

HM: Which isn't very nice of me to myself.

AR: If you know that, could you change that?

HM: I'm trying!

AR: In regards to space, then, is space really important to you? Does Hannah have to write at her writing table, or can Hannah write at her café? Or can she write anywhere, at the bus stop?

HM: I have horrible habits, actually. I have this beautiful ergonomic desk at home from Humanscale, which is fitted to my body or whatever; it's like aerodynamic. It's the future. And I write in bed.

AR: Of course.

HM: I'll go and sit in a coffee shop to get myself started, and I'll sit there and write for a few hours until the coffee's gone cold and my butt hurts. Then I'll get up and go home and get in bed in this position (*demonstrates the worst possible, most dis-ergonomic position in which to sit*). Like the worst possible, dis-ergonomic— It's really stupid. I'll get all wrapped up in my comforter—

AR: But it works for you! You get plays like *Little One*, *This Is War*, you know, you get those plays that come out, so it's clearly working.

HM: I have to trick myself though.

AR: Your audience is loving it.

HM: Well, maybe?

AR: Yes!

HM: I have a propensity— Lately I've actually been feeling like I've been torturing my audience a little bit. I went and saw *This Is War* and *Little One* at the end of their runs and thought, "I got really vicious with audiences." I forgot about their hearts a little bit. I got really mean. And I think I knew I wanted to do that. I think I knew that.

AR: What do you mean, "You knew that"? You said, "I think I got a bit mean, I think I knew that." What did you mean? Did you know you wanted to be mean?

HM: Yeah. I think with *This Is War* in particular I had an understanding in myself that the end result I was looking for from people was to sicken them. Sicken them with the complexity of the situation there but also with what our soldiers are going through when they come back and when they're over there. So I think I knew I was after that reaction, but when I got it I still felt kind of bad. Because it's hard to do that to an audience, to really show them some things and be like: Look. Look at this, motherfuckers.

AR: Hold a mirror up. It's hard in some ways, uncomfortable.

HM: And then you have to live with that as the writer. Did you feel like that with *Brothel #9?*

AR: I did. I really did. That play was such a part of my soul, and continues to be. Oftentimes people from my culture were really mad at me for writing that play and for how uncomfortable it became. I had audience members leave at intermission, leave during the rape scene. They found it too real, they found it too disturbing, but I'm not writing for entertainment. Television is a different thing. For plays I'm not writing to entertain you, I'm writing for it to mean something. So I know that when I'm going in, but you have to do it.

HM: Mm-huh, and then you have to live with the fact that the people who think they are going to see a comedy are gonna be like, "Well, fuck."

AR: But I think by now people know that Hannah Moscovitch and Anusree Roy don't do comedies.

HM: Well, I think we, to our credit—if this is a credit—we both like humour quite a lot in our work.

AR: Yeah. You more than me, though. I find mine is more by default. Your plays, honest to God, I am laughing from top to bottom.

HM: You're sick though.

AR: Even in the most horrific moments there's such a human truth to the writing. Do you know what I mean? Watching one of your plays, I'm thinking: "You're just human. Although you are a Jewish woman in the war and I will never meet you and Hannah made you up, I feel like I know you. And you're pulling up—there's a bun in your vagina." And that's supposed to be somehow funny and I am laughing, but not really. And I feel sick to my stomach that I'm laughing. That is the world you create. But is humour something that you choose to put into your work, or is it something that just comes naturally?

HM: I don't know. I think life is like that, a mix of comedy and tragedy. Lots of people have said that, but if my effort is to show what life is like, comedy's a part of it. There's an authenticity to us joking out of trauma, I think. And I tend to gravitate towards traumatized characters.

AR: Is there a reason you do that?

HM: I don't know. There might be technical reasons, like there's higher drama. Lately I've been thinking about the difference between trauma and experience. Trauma is a more extreme version of experience. But what you're doing with a play is you're asking your character to go through trauma, go through experience for the pleasure of the audience so that they can feel things and be moved, to be that person for a little bit. Feel what that person feels. So it seems like there's a reason why you either choose traumatized characters or that you traumatize your characters over the course of the play. From deep trauma comes humour for many characters.

AR: There has to be for survival in some way.

HM: Yeah, it's part of how you pull yourself up.

AR: We spoke about *This Is War* before and I wanted to congratulate you on your Toronto Critics Award for the play!

HM: Thank you.

AR: I wondered what it feels like to have an award for your play that is "Best Canadian"? In all of Canada *This Is War* is the best. It's not "Best Toronto," it's not "Best GTA," it is "Best Canadian Play." It's not even "Best New Play."

HM: I like the best GTA award.

AR: Best Mississauga Centre! But how does that sit, honestly? The "Best Canadian" title.

HM: I looked at that, actually. I was conscious of it, and I was like, "I think that's a mistake, don't they mean 'Best Toronto'?"

AR: They mean best in Canada.

HM: Did they go everywhere?

AR: That I don't know. But they do mean best in Canada if they're saying "Best Canadian."

HM: What are they talking about? Do they know what they're talking about?

AR: I'm sure they know what they're talking about. I'm really sure they know what they're talking about.

HM: Awards are funny. You have to feel good when you get them, I think, but at the same time it just feels like... At some point it is trivial because what is it? It's just a couple of people making a decision that could have easily gone to any of the other plays this year. I've heard Mordecai Richler, in an interview he gave, say almost the same thing.

AR: But they didn't.

HM: *(laughs)* Well I'm always happy when *you* get awards because I feel like you deserve them. Honestly.

AR: *(laughs)* Thank you. I appreciate that.

HM: Not that I don't feel other people do, but occasionally I'll be like, "Ah," but when you get them I'm like, "Oh yeah, no, I think she's really good too. I think she's very talented."

AR: Thank you. But, back to you, they didn't make a mistake and it wasn't an accident. How does that genuinely feel?

HM: You know what, I am happy about getting the award for that play because I did make a real effort to speak about a part of Canadian experience that has not been talked about a great deal. We had these soldiers who fought this modern desert coalition war and they're a part of our Canadianness, they're part of us, and their experience is not spoken about. We were a nation at war and now we're in a post-war period. This is a period of war art. In many cultures that have been at war, art starts to emerge and there has been kind of a dearth of it here. I think there's more coming now but I felt some sort of odd responsibility to address the topic, actually, which is odd for me because I don't normally write that way. There's this group of people who have been under-represented in the media, and I don't rip things from the headlines normally. When I write, in fact, I tend to set things in the twentieth century, so it was a very different impulse to write that play. And you never know, that feels very new and hard and weird. It was a fucking bitch of a play because it was hard on research. In order to be able to speak about something that was current I had to know it really well.

AR: Writing for *Afghanada* must have helped.

HM: *Afghanada* helped. And I had a lot of access to military consultants because of that. All of that was to say that it's nice to get this award for this play, to get a Canadian award for this play, because it's a play about Canada, addresses something that I felt was part of our Canadianness. So for that reason I was like, "Good." And I feel like Michael Rubenfeld, who is a dear friend, thinks this is the best play I've written, and I don't take that lightly. That was his immediate response. He had seen all my work so I felt like, "Oh good." *(laughs)*

AR: When you're in an intense period of writing, say for *Little One*, which took you from 2009 until 2013 when it went up, do you carry your writing metaphorically with yourself during that time or would that be so many plays that you couldn't function.

HM: I do think about them all—usually in the shower. I just think about them. They're in my head and I rotate in a weird way between them and I'll solve things. I like the process of putting something aside and then just letting my brain work on it. As opposed to trying to solve it. I like the process of standing in the shower and being like, "Oh! That's what's supposed to happen in that story." How do you do it? Do you keep them in your head?

AR: Yes, and it's hard because my content is not always easy. So it hurts my heart because I get so emotional about the people I write about. I take them with me wherever I go, and the shower is a place where a lot of things also get solved. But sometimes I find it hard to the point where I'm like crying all over again for these characters. I get so emotionally attached to somebody or I'll go on their path with them, their journey. The play I'm writing for Factory [Theatre] is about a mental illness, schizophrenia. One of the characters is mentally ill and, oh my God, is it hard to hang out with that play.

HM: It costs you. It costs to write plays.

AR: It really does. Emotionally, it costs you a lot. But you do think it's worth it. Ultimately.

HM: Yeah, I do. Yeah, I do. But it does kind of wreck your day. (laughs)

AR: I feel bad for my family. My poor parents are on this roller coaster with me for every play I write. One of the things I wanted to ask you is, if you were to meet twenty-five-year-old Hannah, what would you say to her?

HM: (thinks) I'd say, "It's gonna be okay." (laughs) I think there were moments in my mid-twenties, right around twenty-five, where I was working at a bar and I would end the night covered in alcohol and lemon peel or whatever, and I'd walk home at 4 a.m. with a wad of dirty money from all of my tips. I remember a moment at the end of one particular night when the bar was a disaster—wine glasses broken everywhere and lemon and lime chunks over everything—and I was covered in beer and thinking, "I'm really not gonna be a writer. I'm really not. (gestures to herself) Obviously not." Because my circumstances were so hard to overcome, imaginatively. And I really wanted to be a writer.

AR: Why?

HM: I have no idea. (laughs) No idea. Maybe I wanted attention, I don't know. I had some idea that I wanted to find my voice in writing and get my voice as a writer. And I had the impulses for writing long before I had any ability. It was all potential. But I really wanted to do it.

AR: Why do you write now?

HM: I imagine sometimes giving it up and it's kind of a romantic fantasy, but it's not real. I don't think I could give it up. I want to do it.

AR: Why?

HM: *(thinks)* It brings meaning to my life. And I cannot imagine my life having meaning without writing. *(laughs)* It's so cheesy.

AR: Absolutely not. I actually 100% agree with you.

HM: I can't imagine giving it up, because then everything goes all dull and grey, like everything loses all of its importance and meaning. Even if I rail against it, which I sometimes do when I get pissy, I don't think I could give it up.

AR: So that was my question about your twenty-five-year-old self. Where do you see yourself at forty-five?

HM: Oh man. I'd love to be able to answer that. For me the future's really... I've been saying blank because I used to say I think the future's really dark but it's not dark. It's just blank. I can't really say.

AR: Twenty-five to here, however old you are, it's not dark. I'd say the lights are damn bright.

HM: Lately I have sort of been in the crucible of trying to work that out, of wondering, "What do I want? What do I want going forward?" And I don't really know. I want to write more plays, and I'm writing on a TV show and a little bit of film. And I'm adapting a novel for the stage and one for film, so I have a bunch of these projects but they feel kind of lateral, like out to the side.

AR: Why, because they have long-term deadlines?

HM: Yeah, and I'm also not sure that they'll go forward. Okay, will you answer it? Where do you want to see yourself when you're forty-five? Maybe you set the template. (*laughter*)

AR: Why do I set the template?

HM: Then I'll know how to answer!

AR: If I'm being completely honest and totally genuine, at forty-five I see myself writing plays that I want to write, authentically, with my own voice. So, continuing to do exactly what I'm doing. I see myself married with children—a big priority for me, and ideals associated with India a lot. I see myself going back home on a regular basis.

HM: Yeah?!

AR: Yeah. Which I do now, so there's a lot of maintaining that I would like to keep. I see myself producing films that are about my own culture and country. And I'll hopefully have these two TV shows that I have ideas for now produced somewhere in my thirties. So that's where I see myself at forty-five. And healthy.

HM: Wow. That's good. That's a great answer.

AR: That's my honest answer.

HM: I know, maybe I'm prevaricating, I can't tell.

AR: If you were to pick an ideal scenario, what would it be? You'd be married because you're engaged to Christian Barry.

HM: I'm engaged. Look at that. (*shows ring*) I'm spending a lot of time right now thinking about being a mother, what that will be.

AR: So it is in your short-term plan?

HM: Yeah, it's in my short-term plan. I think I have a desire, and I can never quite work out what this desire is—if it's megalomania or ambition gone wild or if it's just what writers want—to have my work have a wider reach. I guess that's the impulse towards television in a way because it's a medium that has wide reach.

AR: And are you learning as you're going, or did you know everything about writing for TV when you went in?

HM: My God, I'm learning a ton. Everything is different. How writing happens in television is so different. We sit in a room. You write out loud, first of all. I've never written out loud in my life and I've written in quite a lot of mediums at this point: radio, film, opera, theatre, and I've never written out loud, where you spend eight hours a day sitting and talking about writing. About what you will write, about story, what the storyline will be. And so that's really different. And I've never had to pitch ideas out loud. And some days it's so hard and crazy to do that I feel like I'm having a stroke. The words are coming out in such weird ways because I'm so unused to trying to express intuition and instinct I have towards story and narrative to other people. So it's a pretty intense shift for me anyway, and I'm also introverted, which is why a lot of the mediums I've worked in worked so well for me. But then to be in a room with a lot of other people who are sometimes much more aggressive than you are, and who are talking a lot and loudly and over you, is really different than how I've ever written before. I think it's taking a while for me to understand and to feel safe and to get what the collaboration of it is.

AR: This is your first TV series?

HM: Yeah.

AR: How did you prepare before you went in?

HM: I had no time to prepare because I interviewed and went in within a week.

AR: How did you know what you were doing the first day?

HM: I had no idea, and I have had no idea all the way along. I've been catching up like mad trying to understand anything about the medium. I drive to work with the show runner every day and I quiz him on everything about TV because I have nothing, I'm coming into it with no understanding.

AR: And is it terrifying? Or liberating?

HM: It is terrifying. I was talking to a friend about why people don't learn languages when they become adults, aside from the fact that it's harder neurologically. It's actually very hard psychologically to just feel dumb, and to accept that, "Well, I can't speak this language." It's a bit like that with television, learning a new medium. I'm often like, "Wow, I feel really dumb all the time," like I don't... They're all talking in a vocabulary and a jargon I don't know—I just don't know what they're saying a lot of the time. They'll say, "Oh my God, we've gotta go to pink on this," and I'll be like, "What?"

AR: What does that mean? Do you write that down and then look it up later?

HM: Yeah. So I'll write down a list of terms and then at the end of the day I'll look back at them: "What did that mean, and what did that mean?" And I'm picking my battles. I'll admit some of the time when I don't understand and some of the time I'll just look blankly, like "Mmm huh. Yeah, pink."

AR: Yeah, pink, that's a good colour! I like that colour.

HM: Let's go to pink. And then later I'll be like, "What the fuck did that mean?!" I've learned a lot of new terminology. I've become really obsessed with it. In fact, the show runner accused me of developing my TV vocabulary so I would write a play about TV.

AR: Would you ever do that?

HM: Maybe. (*smiles*)

AR: How was it to have an entire festival at the Tarragon named after you?

HM: (laughs) Well I didn't know they were going to do that. I thought they were just going to produce a bunch of my plays. In fact, I asked my agent specifically if they were going to make a thing about it and he was like, "Nooo."

AR: How could they not make a thing about it, Hannah? They're doing two hundred of your plays in the same season.

HM: Yeah. (laughs) It does make sense. For PR reasons, of course, you would have to explain why you're doing a bunch of plays.

AR: How was it?

HM: I'd had two of my plays go up at once at Factory and even then I felt like I had a lot on the line. And then to have four go up, "Wow, that's great, I have my whole canon on the line." But it feels—all the things you feel— vulnerable... Vulnerable.

AR: Yeah, I hear you.

HM: And you're just trying to put anything in between you and the vulnerability.

AR: Doesn't work.

HM: No, no. You have to feel like it's going to be an extreme experience.

AR: Have you ever felt that a play wasn't ready at opening night?

HM: Yeah, yeah. Oh for sure.

AR: Where does that sit?

HM: Oh my God, it sucks. It feels so bad. You feel sick. Sometimes the worst thing is you know exactly why, and sometimes you don't know why but you have an intuition that it wasn't ready and you're like, "Fuck. Fuck that. Why would I have let that go to production? What possessed me to say yes when I didn't have a draft that I was confident in?"

AR: I've had that once. It's a hard feeling to sit with. "Can't take it back now, can I? And it's opening night."

HM: Yeah. And weirdly I've had plays go up where, for instance, there's been a non-favourable response from critics and friends and I haven't cared because I have liked the play, but then I have had the experience of being praised for work that I didn't think was strong.

AR: Right, amazing what sticks and what doesn't.

HM: Yeah.

AR: Do you feel a pressure for maintaining a reputation and maintaining a standard? So one is public, one is personal. Do you feel a pressure to maintain a reputation publicly, continue to make your work as excellent as the last one, if not more, and the other one is a pressure to maintain the standard that you've created?

HM: That's such a nice… that's really pleasurable for my brain, how you put that. I do feel pressure to maintain both. Oddly enough they are quite divided. I have personal standards; I'll write down a list of these stupid things of what, for me, makes a good play, like one character has an unstoppable desire. I'll write lists of those to get a hold of it for myself, which is, I think, standards, but then I will get concerned, too, about what I'm feeding the audience and if they're going to throw up. And I get concerned about if I'm "changing my brand" too much.

AR: What's your brand?

HM: I don't know. Which is why it's very hard to understand. If you see Judith Thompson's work, her stuff is very recognizable; she has a very strong voice within her work and sometimes I worry I don't. I worry about every possible thing you could worry. I think John Mighton always writes about science and I'll suddenly think, "Maybe that's what I should do! I should just pick something." I always feel like I'm trying to work all that out and that I'm doing it very publicly, like I don't have something that's fully formed. Someone asked me in an interview about that not that long ago: "What's your best play?" and my response was that I don't think I've written it yet.

AR: Really, you feel that?

HM: Yeah, I don't think I've written that play yet.

AR: Why do you feel that?

HM: I don't know. They followed up with, "Well, which play is most you, represents you as a writer?" and I was still like, "I don't know." I don't think I have that play in my canon yet, the one that I think is, "Oh, that's me in a play."

AR: How does it feel to be the fiancé of another creator?

HM: It's beautiful to have someone who understands your work. It's terrifying to not have anyone have a salary.

AR: But you both are doing well for yourselves.

HM: We're doing okay, but it scares the shit out of me. I'm really scared about it. I don't know if it's because my bubby in the Depression... I have no idea what my concerns are about, but I have them. I think there may come a time when people just aren't that interested in my work, and then what will I do? And then I have a fiancé who is in that career too and has the same issues.

AR: What is love?

HM: (thinking, laughs) I honestly just thought of one of Daniel Brooks's plays, where he says that love is learning to live with disappointment.

AR: Amazing. (laughter)

HM: I don't think that's my version of love.

AR: What is your version of love?

HM: Oh my God, I don't know. I was crying to someone stupidly about it the other day over lunch, which is a very awkward time to cry.

AR: I've cried during lunch.

HM: Lunch crying.

AR: I cry during breakfast. Having a soda.

HM: Oh my God. Anyway, it was fine, it was just tearing, it wasn't like wet and ugly. Someone asked me why I'd be in a long-distance relationship and my response was, despite the distance, I love him and I have a vision of my life with him and have a vision of our children and I have a vision of him as a father of those children and I have a vision of us. And while I often don't see my future very clearly, what I can see is him and me old together. I can see us old.

AR: That is more important than anything else.

HM: I don't really see anything else, but I can see that. Despite all the adversity—and I know, I know that if he got sick—I would love him, still, you know? Like I would love him through all the things.

AR: Where do you think that type of love comes from? Is it in knowing someone that deeply, is it in knowing someone's core truth?

HM: I think so! It's funny you say that because I was just thinking, "God, it's so stupid but I do love him more now."

AR: Than you did before?

HM: Yeah. I love him more. And I'm infatuated with him still. But I love him more. Like I look at his face and I'm like, "Oh that's—I love you." When I wake up in the morning and I fall asleep with him. I feel really profound things towards him.

AR: But if you were to say, though, where it came from, for you, would you know?

HM: If I analyzed love for myself I'd say that it comes from curiosity for people and then from a desire to protect them also. Both. Like that deep desire to protect them, if he's sick I want to be there and look after him. I'm very curious about him and what his life path will be, so I guess I need to see it play out and see him as a dad and see what art he'll make and how he'll invent himself as he gets older.

AR: That type of love is really rare. It's so beautiful because you go, "Right, that is the reason why: when you are with somebody, you want to see them through to wherever you get, whatever the end of it is." And I feel that it's rare to have that type of truth, where it goes beyond the superficiality, beyond the career.

HM: Yeah, I think that's quite a nice way of seeing it: "it goes beyond." Because it does. It's not about him having a career or him making me look good.

AR: Exactly, that applies, but…

HM: I'm not saying I look down on that. It's more than the sum of those parts. In the end there's that thing of feeling okay with that person. "Okay" sounds so small but I actually mean you feel solid, grounded, rooted. You feel safe, like they are doing that with you, like you create a charismatic space between the two of you, a small space where the two of you are. And it is such a strange thing, even in friendship, to have that agreement between two people. I do that with those close friends of mine, have that agreement between us where we can look at each other and think, "If you got sick, I would be there," and "If your pregnancy complicates, I will clean your kitchen." And I've had that from friends too. Michael Rubenfeld, when I got very sick, he flew with me to the States to look after me. So you can feel that with friends, too.

AR: That's commitment.

HM: It's that love that goes beyond that you were talking about.

ACKNOWLEDGEMENTS

This Is War was commissioned by The Banff Centre for their seventy-fifth anniversary and was dramaturged by Kelly Robinson and Maureen Labonté. I am very grateful to Kelly Robinson for all of his encouragement and support over the years. Thank you to workshop actors Ari Cohen, Sergio Di Zio, Ian Lake, Sarah McVie, Maev Beaty, Steven Boyle, Kevin Walker, Gregory Prest, Hannah Cheesman, Geoffrey Pounsett, and Stafford Perry, who also acted as dramaturges on the project. Thanks also to Simon Mallett, Sarah Moscovitch, Aaron Rotbard, Christian Barry, Maev Beaty, and Andrew Kushnir, who provided me with informal feedback while I was writing the play. I want to extend thanks to Andrea Romaldi who dramaturged *This Is War* at Tarragon Theatre. I would like to acknowledge the Banff Colony's company of actors of 2010 and 2011 who read the play for me. And I would like to acknowledge the feedback and help I received from the members of the Canadian Forces and the lawyers and war journalists I consulted with over the course of my work on the play, including Scott Taylor, John H Currie, Peter Cuciurean, and Christian Meyknecht. Thank you to the rock star actors who premiered the play: Lisa Berry, Sergio Di Zio, Ari Cohen, and Ian Lake. Thanks to actors John Cleland, Brendan Murray, and Kevin Walker for touring Tarragon's premiere production to Prairie Theatre Exchange in Winnipeg. Immense thanks are due to Richard Rose for collaborating with me on the development of *This Is War* at Tarragon Theatre.

My thanks are due to the following documentaries: *Operation Homecoming: Writing the Wartime Experience, Restrepo, Wartorn, Alive Day Memories, Hell and Back Again, Obama's War, Inside Afghanistan, The Battle for Marjah, Taking on the Taliban, Jack: A Soldier's Story, Wounded* (from the BBC), *Taxi to the Dark Side, Our War: 10 Years in Afghanistan, Fighting the Taliban, Meeting the Taliban, Exit Afghanistan, Afghan Massacre: The Convoy of Death, Fixer: The Taking of Ajmal Naqshbandi, Afghanistan: The Forgotten War, The Invisible War, Sister in Arms,* and *Why We Fight.* ·

My thanks are due to the following works of non-fiction and photojournalism: *Infidel* by Tim Hetherington; *War is a Force that Gives us Meaning* by Chris Hedges; *War* by Sebastian Junger; *Outside the Wire: The War in Afghanistan in the Words of its Participants*, edited by Kevin Patterson and Jane Warren; *The Savage War: The Untold Battles of Afghanistan* by Murray Brewster; and *Afghanistan: A Military History from Alexander the Great to the War Against the Taliban* by Stephen Tanner.

Thanks also to the war photographer Louie Palu for talking to me about his experiences in Afghanistan and referring me to his website. And thanks to the online Canadian Forces real combat footage.

Hannah's writing for the stage includes *Essay*, *The Russian Play*, *East of Berlin*, *The Mill Part II: The Huron Bride*, *The Children's Republic*, *Little One*, and *In This World* (for young audiences). Her plays have been produced across the country, including at the Tarragon Theatre in Toronto, where she is currently playwright-in-residence, Factory Theatre, Alberta Theatre Projects, Manitoba Theatre Centre, Great Canadian Theatre Company, and the Magnetic North Theatre Festival. Hannah's work has won multiple Dora Awards and she's been nominated for the Governor General's Literary Award, the Carol Bolt Award, and the international Susan Smith Blackburn Prize. Hannah is a graduate of the National Theatre School of Canada and attended the University of Toronto.